POWER

- Power in use is the ability to cause an event to happen or not to happen. It is the ability to influence or control events and people.

- Power equals control. Control means fewer surprises, greater input into decisions, and greater predictability in the work place.

POWER IS INSEPARABLE FROM THE PEOPLE WHO HAVE IT.

POWERBASE
How to Build It
How to Keep It

POWERBASE
How to Build It
How to Keep It

MARILYN MOATS KENNEDY

FAWCETT CREST • NEW YORK

A Fawcett Crest Book
Published by Ballantine Books
Copyright © 1984 by Marilyn Moats Kennedy

Library of Congress Catalog Card Number: 83-24431
ISBN 0-449-20750-1
This edition published by arrangement with Macmillan Publishing Company

Manufactured in the United States of America

First Ballantine Books Edition: May 1985

For Anne Evelyn Kennedy
and Daniel J., of course!

ACKNOWLEDGMENTS

I want to thank three people who truly made this book possible. Donna Reimer, my associate at Career Strategies, has spent countless hours working with me on this project and juggling other parts of the business while I wrote. Janet Goldman Shlaes, my editor/researcher, spent much time editing and organizing. Without their yeoman efforts I would still be working on this project. My agent, Jane Jordan Browne, gave excellent support and feedback.

I have also received help from the Wilmette and Evanston public libraries and the Northwestern University library. The staffs there have been very helpful in suggesting ways to verify facts.

Career Strategies' clients have made a tremendous (although anonymous) contribution to this book. They have shared their stories, their successful and unsuccessful tactics, and most important, their conclusions. They are the ones who pointed up the victim syndrome and the general lack of knowledge in this area.

Finally, my husband Daniel and daughter Anne Evelyn have been very patient while I spent months hunched over the word processor, all but ignoring them.

CONTENTS

CONTENTS

PREFACE

When a group of people who are having career problems get together, their version of events is often similar. They believe they are being done in and done to. The world, at least the piece of it in their offices, is out to get them. It is not their fault; it is the system. What can they do? At no time do they see themselves as participants in that system—only as its victims. That attitude is both unrealistic and a real block to career advancement.

This book exists because no one needs to be a victim if he or she does not choose to be. The process of being victimized depends, at least in the office, on agreeing to play the role of victim. For instance, if someone disdains participation in the grapevine and off-site socializing, both universal in offices, he or she is agreeing to play the victim's role.

In years of career planning with clients one fact stands out. Most people, while longing for power, are looking for a way to short-circuit the power-building process. They want power but not the burden of having to work to build it. That cannot be. If you are to become more powerful, you must spend about a third as much time on power building as you spend on actually doing your job. Only if you build that time into your schedule and make peace with the fact that you need and will court power can you protect and advance your career. Fight the system, however much you disagree with it, and you handicap yourself. No matter how much you hate the system, it exists and must be reckoned with. Furthermore, no one can make you powerful but yourself. The company cannot give you power. It gave you a position and an opportunity to build a base. The rest is up to you.

As you read this book it should become clear that you need to think about power as part of work, not something separate from it. Getting the job done, getting the result, depends on understanding the system and making it work for you. Unfortunately, being a victim is, more than anything else, a very comfortable role. It is both a reason and an excuse for doing nothing.

As you read this book you will be faced with many choices. Will you become an active participant in power building, and if so, how will you do it? Will you choose to use power for career advancement or to keep the position you have? Will power help you maximize job satisfaction or just build self-esteem? The hardest choices will always be those that involve trading off your desire to get even or to tell someone your "honest" opinion or to show off with your need to build and maintain relationships with the patently unlikeable. To make those choices will test your real desire to be powerful.

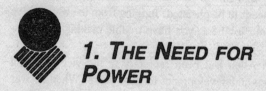

1. THE NEED FOR POWER

WHEN Mary Anne Elkins (all names have been changed) was fired from a Fortune "500" company, she was totally surprised. She had four years of excellent reviews and better than average raises. As manager of the word processing department she had watched her staff increase from ten to thirty, including two supervisors. At the showdown her boss was apologetic but firm. "We need someone who understands power and can use it effectively. You don't. You're too accommodating to those you like even though they really can't help us build the overall operation or the department's reputation. You punish those you dislike even if they can," she said.

In less than two years Bill Morgan moved up from supervisor of the bank's teller line to head cashier. He was, in his own eyes, a "comer." He was finishing his MBA at night and believed he would soon be able to transfer to the commercial banking area. Three weeks after he received the MBA degree he met with his boss. He explained he wanted to be a calling officer. The boss said that although he liked Bill personally, he felt his skills were better suited to some part of operations, possibly the credit card area. "Calling officers," the boss said, "need a feel for who is important, who should be cultivated in an organization, and who just needs to be placated. Judging from the way you've handled your job here, you have trouble making those distinctions."

Elsbeth Allen had been secretary to the vice-president for research and development for five years. When he was named chief executive officer (CEO), she expected to move with him. Imagine her surprise when another woman, several years older and, in Elsbeth's opinion, less presentable, was named his secretary. When she asked her former boss why he had not taken her along, he hedged. Finally he said, "Elsbeth, you just don't understand the way things work here. You're bright. You are very competent technically, but you're not very savvy. That's the one thing a CEO's secretary must be."

These people have one thing in common. They do not understand how power works in organizations. Of the three, not one understands what his/her relationship to the power structure is or should be. Power is not even something they can fantasize about with any skill. They do not realize, or at least appear not to realize, that everybody who works needs power. An independent power base in the organization is critical to survival. Being able to build and use power is always part of getting the job done. Depend entirely on the position power that comes with the job, and you could be out. Build your own base, and you are likely to move up or hold on. At least you will have choices.

Power building has never been more important than it is

right now; yet you won't find courses on how to do it in any business school curriculum. Given a permanently uncertain economy with structural changes taking place in many industries, slow or no growth in many companies, and more people competing for fewer management openings, learning to build and maintain power is often more important to job success than hard work and a reputation for productivity.

Although they do not see it that way, people who disdain power tend to victimize themselves with enthusiastic monotony. It's unlikely Mary Anne, Bill, or Elsbeth will identify a lack of savvy about power as a major career problem. It is much more likely each will nurse a feeling of having been wronged. How comfortable it is to blame the system and see oneself as a helpless but virtuous victim! Each will get another job only to face a similar situation because power is the one constant in every work place. Whether it is a Fortune "500" company or the "Ma and Pa" laundromat down the street, power exists, is distributed and redistributed, and is an object of controversy and concern. Whatever people say, they want power in the work place even more than they want money.

WHAT POWER IS

Ask people to define power, and they will talk about "clout"—that infamous word for influence punctuated with brass knuckles. Others mention the sinister aspects of power, such as backstabbing and backbiting. For them power and its uses are to be feared. They see themselves as "done in and done to." For most people power defies analysis and common sense. Unless you know what is going on, watching people vie for power in the office will seem to be a happening without rules or logic.

Power—especially as it is used in the work place—is one of the most fascinating and least understood processes that anyone can explore seriously. The pursuit of power influences behavior more than the desire for money, the drive to excel, the desire for results, and the restraint of ethics combined. Although the public image of power is often a negative one, even people who can not define power recognize and respect it. Let us look at the two basic qualities of power in the work place.

1. Power in use is the ability to cause an event to happen or not to happen. It is the ability to influence or control events and people and, in both real and office politics, to influence how events are interpreted. Power can, but need not be, part of the delegated authority. Some power may come with the job, although it is very possible to have the right to command others without the power to force compliance. People may not understand how power and authority diverge until they are put into a situation in which the authority given by the boss, and confirmed by the job description, is not enough to do the job.

How can that happen? Often what the job requires is the skill to influence peers and subordinates, not the right to command them. No boss or job description can make a person influential or cause others to cooperate. Positions are as static as the boxes on an organizational chart; it is the person on the job who influences and cooperates with other people. The person doing the job must build and maintain relationships if he or she is to get the work done.

2. Power equals control. Even those who don't know why they are interested in power instinctively know they want and need more control over their careers. Control

means fewer surprises, greater input into decisions, and greater predictability in the work place. People who seek power are often looking for ways to secure themselves or their jobs within a changing environment—which is what every work place is. We may ask if that is possible or desirable, but we can't doubt that many people are motivated by the desire to control their work and their lives.

Job security is not the same thing as control. It is possible to have job security without either influence or control. Teachers and civil servants are perfect examples. Paternalistic companies also provide many instances of job security divorced from any kind of influence.

Most people do not expect to gain total control of their work lives; they just want ever-increasing influence within the organization. In their zeal for more control, they may easily confuse power building with office politics. While power is part of the political process, it can not be explained solely by the political realities of organizational life. Office politics involves people rubbing egos as they get the work out. Power building is much more subtle and complex. Real power is very different from command or position power. Both of those are given by the organization. What makes power so desirable is that people can get and use it even when they lack both position and command power. Think of the secretaries you have known with enormous influence, the sales people whose sales figures protected them, or the people whose pleasing personalities allowed them to do things forbidden to others.

THE CHARACTERISTICS OF POWER

Although power has many forms and as many faces as the people using it, there are some identifiable characteristics of power as it is used in work situations. Power is inseparable from the individuals who have it. A company, department, or office is only as powerful as the people who populate it, and then only if they want to be powerful. For example, data processing departments can be forces to be reckoned with or simply groups of timorous servants buffeted by powerful users. This is the major difference between power in the work place and political power. The office of president of the United States is powerful, regardless of the name of the occupant. However, even the president can and does make the office more or less powerful by his individual approach. In work places, the individual is more than seventy-five percent of the equation. Even someone called president or CEO can be powerless if he or she rejects power as a primary management tool.

If you analyze some recent business failures from a power viewpoint, you will discover power vacuums. A power vacuum occurs when someone with the power to act refuses to use that power. For instance, the CEO of an electronics company goes off on a tangent pursuing the perfect microchip and lets his subordinates run the show. He is not physically absent, just mentally removed from the organization's day-to-day operation. When he returns to reality, he finds the business in Chapter Eleven, attempting to reorganize and stave off bankruptcy. Naturally he then has less power and must struggle harder to gather back what has moved by default to his subordinates. He has to remind his aides that he wants to see the budget before it is finalized and that he expects to be consulted on the marketing plan. They have made all the big decisions while he has "been away." There is no question that this is terrible management, but it is even worse from a CEO's power building and maintenance perspective. However, it was good power building by his subordinates; they saw opportunities and used them to their advantage. When the business fails, they will have learned enough to move to higher-level positions elsewhere.

Power always has a source. There is no such thing as free-floating power. If you locate the source or sources of someone's power, you can change, reshape, or even destroy it. If you don't know the source, however, you are helpless. Janet, an inept but attractive data processing manager, gets a much larger than average annual raise. Her peers wonder why. Who made the decision, and who is protecting and advancing her career? The speculation is that Janet and her boss's superior are "involved"; but the grapevine is not entirely certain. About half of her peers are saying it is true, but others disagree. Nothing can be done to reduce Janet's power until the source of it is positively identified. If people take swipes at Janet without knowing her power source, they will weaken themselves and provoke retaliation instead. They will appear to be victimizing Janet, and even some of her would-be critics will not tolerate that.

Power is assumed. People have power when they grasp and use it. If a manager causes someone who is not within his formal control to act, that is power. If someone acts out of fear, respect, friendship, or just an inability to refuse, the person who received the service and caused the action is powerful. Power can be transferred from person to person, but not intact and not against someone's will. For instance, if a department is managed by someone who is very interested in building and using power, and he or she is replaced by someone with little interest in anything but the work, the power which is not assumed by the new manager will either be lost or spread among others in the department.

Role power usually comes with a job. If a manager does not make the decisions necessary to demonstrate his/her strengths, others will make those decisions—haphazardly. If a man supervises ten people but refuses to put any position distance between himself and his subordinates, he is refusing to assume the role power of his position. His refusal to distance himself from his subordinates invites them to impose on the relationship. They may slack off in their work, or they may manipulate him emotionally. What they won't do, however, is have the same relationship with him that they would have with a manager who clearly intended to exercise the power of his/her role.

Power may be redistributed by theft or the lack of a spirited defense. A competitive department can grab power by doing something better or more quickly than the department originally assigned the job. Users of the necessary service will now feel free to choose the competitive department if it better fulfills their needs. There is rarely a traffic cop in such situations. If one person or group gets more power, the other person or group is left with less. If the department that lost power does not seem to react, it sends a signal to everyone watching that there is no defense. This struggle occurs frequently in organizations with fuzzy departmental lines. Does the job belong to marketing or sales promotion? If marketing does the better job, they will soon get requests to do things that sales promotion used to do.

Power often evokes fear and respect, not to mention

envy! Power without fear is a contradiction in terms. This is probably one of its most uncomfortable characteristics. If people observe that someone does not use his or her power, they automatically assume that the person has none. After all, if you do not discipline those who cross you, is there any explanation other than that you lack the power to do so? It is unthinkable that you would choose not to defend your turf. This is a major problem in power building for many people. Even if someone acquires the ability to create fear, influence people, or control events, will that person choose to do so? More people fail at power building because they would rather be powerless and loved than be powerful and feared.

Power must have observable consequences for people. If the effects cannot be seen, the person presumed to be powerful is actually powerless. Consider the problems of people who have formal titles but lack authority to make decisions or changes. Minorities and women in the sixties and seventies often faced this problem. A woman got the title, an office, and a respectable salary, but was not given the power to command, control, or change. She was firmly under the control of her superior, however much she would have liked to believe otherwise. If the trappings of power are especially rich, the person thus surrounded may not see her own powerlessness for months or even years.

This can happen to anybody, male or female. If your boss says, "Listen, Bill, just run that report by me before you send it out," one of two things is happening: Either the boss is interested and simply wants to see how you have handled the assignment or, if you really do not have the formal power you thought, he or she is acting as a censor. You do not really have the power to send out the report without the boss's approval.

Power is very sexy. Henry Kissinger once said, "Power is the ultimate aphrodisiac." He was right. It is a cachet for both men and women. Women who will never decorate the fashion pages of *Glamour* or *Vogue*, but are nonetheless savvy about power, are professionally and personally sought after. It is accepted without question that an aggressive, unattractive man with power will attract female admirers. Office romances often result from the intense feelings that power building and power grabbing provoke. When someone's engines are already in fourth gear, anything can happen.

Power has no emotional or ethical content. Power is neutral; it is neither good nor bad. All ethical choices are made by the person using power. There are no built-in ethics. Those who pursue power develop their own ethical standards or work within those set by the organizational culture. Do not interpret this to mean that all or even any powerful people lack ethics. The desire for power is not an ethical problem; the trouble lies in how power is used. For most powerful people motive is not as important as results. A person whose motives are murky may be very powerful so long as he or she gets results; that is, people can see power, wielded with intent, producing the desired effect.

Self-publicity done through the grapevine enhances power. This is an important characteristic of power. No one can be powerful in an organization strictly because of the esteem of others. Publicity by others may enhance power, but self-publicity is more effective. People who merchandise themselves inevitably have more power than those who wait to be "discovered." Putting oneself forward, however, is rarely pleasant and never comfortable. There is always a risk that others will seek to tarnish the reputations of the powerful.

Power must be protected. Many people begin a job with

position power. If they do not protect it, they will soon lose it. For power is like quicksilver: It moves very quickly and is hard to hold on to. Possession is the ultimate law. If a manager says to a subordinate, "Jack, you make that decision," Jack will do as he is told. Unless the manager specifically says, "Jack, you make that decision just this once," a part of the manager's real power will be transferred to Jack, although neither the manager's nor Jack's position in the hierarchy has changed.

The best example of the impermanence of power is the CEO who loses his power base as he nears retirement. At sixty, his views are still important to the senior vice-presidents just below him. At sixty-four, people are either guessing who his successor is likely to be or, if they already know, taking the successor's views very seriously. The CEO may be asked for an opinion, but the heir apparent's views will dominate. The CEO's job description, position, and salary have not changed. Had he not told everyone exactly whenhe would leave, he might have been powerful longer. He might also, had he worked at it, kept his influence stronger until he actually stepped down. The CEO of an advertising agency knew the office was rife with rumors that he would be stepping down two years from now. Instead of letting people know whom he had chosen as his successor, he heated up the grapevine with the news that there were three candidates. (In fact, he was still somewhat ambivalent about his choice, so he wasn't lying.) He regularly interviewed outside people whom the troops would consider hot prospects. He looked perplexed whenever the agency management committee met. None of the internal candidates for the top spot felt able to press the CEO because nothing seemed firm. No one seemed truly an insider. Not until three months before he announced his retirement did he name his successor. That is smart power management.

But you can reduce even significant power by hesitant or indifferent use. Create the impression that you might not use your power, regardless of the quantity you possess, and you will have relinquished it. Power demands action. Robbed of action, even position power is worthless. For instance, if a boss has the power to fire people at will but declares frequently that he would never do so, he has given away his power to fire anyone. It will be almost impossible for him to exercise that authority, however much he might need to do so to correct a problematic situation.

Power shifts internally with every change or rumor of change. If someone counts primarily on position power or a job title, he or she will be regularly disappointed; job titles are a joke in organizational life. Remember all of the senior secretaries who are now called administrative assistants even though they serve more often than they assist? Even salary grade levels have little to do with the real power structure. For instance, a scientist may be paid more than a vice-president, but at the same time he is unable to order his own office supplies without his manager's signature on the requisition.

Power requires regular maintenance. It is impossible to talk about anyone with a permanent power base; it is possible only to talk about the quality of someone's present base. People who talk about what they have done "for years" tend to be less powerful than those who speak only in the present tense. Why? As business conditions change, those who meet the new conditions readily acquire more power. Those who are stymied or slowed by change have diminished power. Money does not constitute a permanent base unless money is regularly used to build power. For example, a salesman who impresses his clients with lavish spending loses his clout when he stops spending.

Power building is fun; it is challenging, exciting, and at times dangerous. Most people enjoy the byplay and the conspiratorial building of alliances. And they work harder at their jobs and find power building increases their work satisfaction.

THE SOURCES OF POWER

If organizational charts and job descriptions do not accurately describe organizational power, then where is it and where does it come from? Power rests on a three-legged base, the legs of which are research, relationships, and resources.

1. *Research* is the first leg. You have heard that knowledge is power. That is only partially true. The knowledge that constitutes power in organizations is research into what people think, say, and do, not book learning or expertise. In this contest, the reporter moves ahead of the scholar. Knowing how to do something is not as important as knowing who has certain kinds of information and how to get them to share. In power building, the kind of knowledge that we are interested in is twofold: Who are the powerful people? What is the source of their power? Even someone inexperienced at power building—for instance, a new worker in his or her twenties—would be able to shorten the learning curve by recognizing the dominant position of internal information, née gossip, in the power structure. The research that produces information—and verifies it—is a product of both skill and diligence. People with good research skills

can plan, predict events accurately, form alliances, and trade information. They can do all of this while holding seemingly low-level jobs. Power building is a democratic process; everyone can play.

Knowing the vital role information plays, it is hard to imagine a company CEO who would choose to get all of his information through subordinates and still expect to maintain his power. Even if he were high-minded, he ought to expect that his subordinates might color the facts for their own protection or benefit. Richard Nixon did not make that assumption and paid dearly for it. CEOs who know and understand the relationship between research and power are unlikely to give subordinates that kind of leverage. They will have coffee with people throughout the organization and preserve an independent judgment, thereby providing an incentive for subordinates to pass on the news reasonably unembellished. By being part of the informal as well as the formal systems, they can work through whichever is situationally most effective. If they have only command to rely on, they will be able to do only those things in the realm of the formal system.

2. *Relationships* are the second leg. Power rests on relationships with others. For most people, working effectively becomes a constant struggle to fulfill one's obligations while extracting quid pro quo from others. This is the most important leg of your power base. If your information gathering is faulty, you can still be powerful if you learn to build and maintain critical relationships. Relationships rest on one important base: Every relationship established must be mutually beneficial. The rallying cry of the powerful is: "What can I do for you so you will want to do it my way?" It is not: "How can I force you to do it my way?" Relationships

are designed for mutual benefit. If they were not resources, why would anyone want them?

3. The final leg is *resources*. In order to get information and build relationships, you need some organizational resources. For most people the primary resource is a job title which legitimizes their participation in the system. Resources may also include budget influence or control. Money, although important, is much less so in power building than research and relationships. If one has information and relationships, financial resources are fairly easy to acquire. A financially rich manager would not be able to turn those resources into influence without information and contacts. For example, the purchasing agent in a company may or may not be powerful. While he or she is supposed to control the purchase of materials and approve budgets, a line manager who wants a particular good or service may choose to circumvent the purchasing agent. If his or her relationships are strong enough, the purchasing agent, unhappy with this action, will retaliate, thereby warning others not to try the same thing. The purchasing agent may "mix up" the order or "lose" it temporarily. This kind of vindictiveness has its dangers; people may think the agent actually made a mistake! Without strong relationships, staff people will always be forced to acknowledge the superior position of line people.

Often the job itself cannot supply enough financial resources or an important enough title to make someone powerful. He or she will always be dependent on research and relationships to get the work out even in the best run organizations. Jobs, once designed, are formally reviewed and restructured infrequently—it is both disrupting and tedious to do so. However, most people will, if only mentally, re-create and regularly rewrite their own job descriptions. Sometimes people will act out what they want rather than what they have been assigned. This accounts for some of the power dislocations in jobs.

Given the nature of power, the alternatives become very clear. You either become a power builder, with all of the work that entails, or you duck. If you duck, you will not necessarily save yourself from trouble because someone may be stalking you as his prey at this very moment! You will, however, be spared the effort involved in day-to-day power building. You will also fly seat-of-the-pants through every crisis. It is not a pretty picture—but it is the alternative to power building.

If you become a power builder you will have a sense of control over your own working life. You will know fewer cold sweats and fewer moments of helpless rage resulting from an inability to get people and things to work your way. As one engineer said, after reluctantly getting involved with power building in his department, "At least nothing comes as a complete surprise. If the company were to go under next week or my boss were to be fired, it's likely that with my resources within and outside the company, I'd have some advance notice in order to plan my response. I used to think that too many people died in those western shoot-outs. Now I'm firmly in favor of ambushes. At least they can be planned!"

2. FINDING THE POWER IN ORGANIZATIONS

MARTHA Orange was second in command in corporate communications for a very large insurance company. Her boss, June, a woman with a talent for swishing a business skirt, was always telling Martha that when she moved up Martha would get her job. Martha worked hard, effectively and, alas, naively. June had long since let top management know that while only forty, she had extra-curricular interests. A vice-presidency with the company was not her goal. She told Martha she was panting to move ahead. Martha might still be supporting June had she not begun to look at the power structure in the department.

When she analyzed what was going on, it was as if someone had sent her a memo outlining the situation; it was that clear. Martha was making all of the day-to-day decisions in the department. She had the firmest and warmest media connections, approved the brochures and newsletters, and sweated over the annual report. Everyone in the department treated her as the boss. True, June was spending her time on political games—but not the right ones. She was not aiming at moving up; she was working toward on-the-job retirement. Martha decided that since she was taking the risks and making the decisions, without any prospects for advancement, she ought to pursue the title and money elsewhere. She got another job. June gave her a Tiffany paperweight and wept real tears at her going-away party. Since June would now have to work for a living, at least until she found another Martha, her grief was genuine.

Martha did not realize early on that even if June had the title, she didn't necessarily use the power that went with it. Martha, by making the decisions and doing the work, had usurped June's power, albeit with June's complicity.

Dick went to his boss eight weeks before his performance review. He had prepared excellent arguments, all well documented, to show why he should get an above-average raise this year. He was very convincing. His boss reacted favorably, admiring both Dick's logic and his diligence. Dick had not exaggerated his worth to the company; he was clearly underpaid. Dick's boss said he was convinced.

Two months later the boss called Dick in and said, "Dick, you did an outstanding job this year. I fought for you, and you're getting a five percent salary increase." Dick was stunned. Instead of the ten percent to twelve percent he had anticipated—or, more accurately, counted on—he was getting the standard increase.

How could that have happened? Dick did everything by the book. He did more work than his co-workers, ninety-eight percent of whom would get a five percent raise. They did nothing except stay on the payroll. Many did not perform particularly well—calling their work adequate would stretch the point. Dick's boss even liked him better than the others in the department. Why hadn't he been rewarded? Here is what went wrong.

Dick used the formal system; he worked through the chain of command. He didn't know two things (knowable only through the informal system) that were critical to his success.

1. His boss did not make final salary decisions. He merely recommended increases to his boss. She made the decision even though she knew nothing firsthand about Dick's work.

2. Salary decisions were made six months before he even talked with his boss. While the cement on those decisions had not quite dried, it was still nearly set. (In fairness, it would have been difficult for Dick's boss to tell him that he did not have the power to act. But the grapevine would have known!)

Tom Jackson, the manager of research and development for a small computer software firm, tried to get his departmental budget approved. He talked with his boss, Lloyd, the vice-president for product development. Lloyd could not help him. He tried the comptroller. Mary Margaret did not really think that she could approve it. He thought about talking with the president of the company, some three thousand miles away. Tom felt as if he were looking for the Wizard of Oz. He had followed the yellow brick road, but Oz was nowhere to be found. He continued to spend money as needed. It made him feel uncomfortable, but no one else seemed to care. It was business as usual. Tom later learned that he had unknowingly followed the informal system. No one cared about budget approvals as long as the firm made money.

What is going on in these cases? There must be power within the company. Why is it so hard to find and tap the source? Because, while there is power in an organization, it is diffused. In order to find the real power for permission, to consult with, or simply to use, you have to know where to look. You might have more power than you think, if you analyze the situation! Therefore, it is important to analyze how power is distributed throughout the company. To do that you must be able to recognize where the power is.

WHERE POWER IS

You know where power is supposed to be in organizations. That is obvious: Organizations are like pyramids, and power always moves from top to bottom. The trouble starts when you try to make the system work as promised. You have gone through the proper channels, fired off memos, read the company policy manual, and waited. When nothing happens, you get frustrated. If you are young, you may think that it was something you did or did not know enough to do. Maybe your technique was not right. Only after you have worked for five or ten years do you realize that you were (and maybe still are) looking for the wrong thing in the wrong place. The power you wanted and needed was never part of the formal system. Therefore, all your efforts to bend or influence the formal system were wasted.

Every company has two power systems, the formal and the informal. The formal system is the process by which owners and/or top management delegate responsibilities, and the power to meet those responsibilities, to layers of management and ultimately to the individual workers below them on the organization chart. This is not done uniformly even when people have exactly the same titles and responsibilities. Delegated power does not flow neatly through the organization.

Imagine a finite amount of power flowing like a river from the top of the pyramid to the bottom. As the river goes by, vice-presidents and then managers dip in and take some power out. This reduces the amount remaining in the river. At each level of management individuals take out whatever they think, or have been told, they are entitled to. If they can, some may take more. By the time the river flows by the average worker, it is almost dried up. However, as the river continues to flow some people, through lack of use, put some of their power back. That power is now available for someone else to take.

The informal system is always the stronger, more inclusive, and more efficient one. Formal power flows only in one direction. It does not move up the ladder (that is, supervisors cannot give managers power). Therein lies the weakness that creates and sustains the informal system. How can people influence or control others as they move up the pyramid? If power moved formally both up and down, there would be no need for an informal system because everything could be done through formally designated channels.

Top management expects that through organizational charts, chain of command, job descriptions, prescribed relationships, and other internal controls, power will move through the organization as originally intended. It rarely does. If power could be controlled and accounted for, as money is, organizational life would be significantly simpler and infinitely more rational. It cannot. That is why top management, however controlling, can provide only broad outlines of how power is to be distributed. The formal system depends on people knowing and accepting their places in the organizational hierarchy. In fact, the workers make the power allocations, and continue making them, through the informal system.

THE FORMAL SYSTEM

The formal system can be defined, structured, redefined, and reworked on paper. There are even written sanctions. If someone openly breaches the formal system, he or she can be disciplined or fired, although this is truer in theory than in practice. Most firings occur for purely political reasons, not because someone failed to honor the formal system. Here are some of the most common identifying marks of the formal system.

1. The principal tool of the formal system is the written organization chart. Next is the job description. Fact: Job descriptions are never accurate. They are fences around tasks usually meant to warn people about territorial boundaries. The more importance a company attaches to job descriptions, the more important will be the informal system for getting things done.

2. The formal system is a fallback system. Only when the informal system fails (that is, when cooperation breaks down and people become territorial) do we look to the rules. Most work is accomplished, and most relationships are established, through the informal system. Even if job descriptions mandate that people work together, the formal system will detail only reporting relationships. The working relationships will be established informally as people decide whose help they need or want.

3. The formal system can only be changed formally. That means the documents that sustain it have to be rewritten and usually reapproved through the chain of command. This makes the formal system slow and cumbersome. It also makes the system very political because so many people must get involved in order to protect their own interests and get their ideas into the formal record. In some companies

entire committees labor intensively and continuously at re-working the formal system.

4. The formal system exists solely to provide a sense of direction and the security of a visible structure. It also re-assures bankers, accountants, and stockholders that a gen-uine organization exists. It cannot, however, be used for either delicate negotiations or complicated deals. As people try to make the formal system do more than it can (for example, loosely hold together the frame of the organiza-tion), they will cause the system to display its flaws and weaknesses. This produces an "Emperor's New Clothes" syndrome. As you may recall, the child who pointed out that the emperor was actually naked was not particularly popular. His elders tried to ignore him. In a modern cor-poration no one would expose the emperor's nakedness. If people point out weaknesses and flaws in the formal power structure, they are breaking the unwritten rules that clearly state: "Honor, but do not depend on, the formal structure."

For example, it would be too blatant to write a memo to someone's boss asking for his or her help on a project without having checked through the informal system to see how the person you wanted was likely to react. If you use only the formal system, you invite retaliation through the informal system. Suppose Mary, to whose boss you had written the memo, did not want to be borrowed. Even though the formal system said that was possible, Mary might feel her rights had been violated. Checking with her and ar-ranging things between you and then using the formal system to ratify would make more sense. If you borrowed Mary without any acknowledgement of formal procedure, that is too far in the other direction. There is a balance.

5. The formal structure reflects top management's values and fantasies. Knowledge of the formal structure is helpful

in deducing what top management's ideas and dreams were when the company was initially established. A policy statement does not describe reality; it addresses an idealized organization. Sometimes the formal structure, and the way that it has changed over the years, tells a lot about the crises the company has faced. Reorganizations and restructurings always reveal how things have been changed.

THE INFORMAL SYSTEM

Contrast this with the informal system. Under the informal system relationships are fluid. Things get done across organizational lines rather than within them.

1. Everybody can function as an equal in the informal system, no matter where he or she sits on the organizational chart. The janitor may be treated with more respect than a manager if that is what it takes to get him to perform. A reluctant janitor might be disciplined through the formal system, but that takes time, reduces everyone's morale, and may produce malicious compliance. It is much easier to meet his need for attention and to get on with the work, especially for those who may want special favors from him in the future.

2. All relationships within the informal system are negotiated. Nobody does anything for nothing or purely to help the team. Nobody owes anybody anything just because of his or her position on the organizational chart. All relationships are deliberately created. The formal system may throw people together, but it cannot force them to cooperate with one another.

3. All business is conducted by adapting the formal system to fit the current crisis. The informal system is always used to solve crises and resolve political problems because to acknowledge political problems formally is taboo. Deal-

ing with a personality problem between peers requires delicate negotiations, not a rereading of formal job descriptions or company policy.

4. Informal power is always used face to face, not on paper. A deal may be confirmed later in writing, but all negotiations are initially handled orally and in person. The quickest way to lose power is to not perform exactly as you agreed to.

5. The ethics of the informal system are much more rigid than those of the formal system. The informal system will not accept excuses because there is no way to enforce informal agreements formally. Reprisals are invariably taken.

6. Ultimately it is the informal system that makes the company work. People need extraordinary, not formal, cooperation to get the work out. You can test this assumption yourself. Look at your job description and also at those of your peers and subordinates. If each of you only does exactly what he or she is supposed to do, according to your job descriptions, the company will eventually fail. People doing exactly what they are paid to do is rarely enough. Companies get into trouble when they reward people who use only the formal system. A financially or managerially troubled company can be identified by the number of people lovingly clutching job descriptions and organized into a Greek chorus chanting, "It's not my job." (This is one of the reasons that government at all levels is in trouble.)

7. The informal system is not and can never be publicly acknowledged. To let people know that the informal system is more important than the formal one is forbidden. Waves of insecurity sweep through an organization when people openly begin to breach the formal system. If top management says, "Listen, we know about the informal system. We know the inmates are really running the asylum," morale

and productivity will bottom out. I know and you know, but "we" do not know officially. Many new managers, once they have discovered the informal system, nearly sink themselves by talking openly about what they have learned.

8. The informal system operates like a club. If someone ignores it, he or she is denied membership. There are no other requirements for membership and no dues except reciprocity. Being able to deliver research, relationships, or resources is the key.

9. The informal system becomes harder to penetrate as you move up the corporate ladder. A CEO is always in danger of being cut off from the informal information going through the organization because subordinates will try to increase their own power and political advantage by "protecting" the boss from unpleasant news, that is, the facts. The test of a CEO's effectiveness is his or her ability to penetrate these barriers and to use the informal system.

10. The most important part of the informal system is the grapevine. The grapevine carries news and reactions to the news. Without the kind of factual, uncensored news transmitted through the grapevine, power is impossible to build or hold. Anyone who hears only the official news (that which is written or "officially" pronounced) cannot do his/her job effectively for very long. Official news is deliberately packaged to produce an effect. It answers only the question "what" but not "how" or "why." It is also old news by the time it hits the formal channels.

While formal channels may carry the fact that there was a meeting of the board of directors today, the grapevine will carry impressions of the meeting, speculations on what might happen as a result of the meeting, and also what any individual thought or is planning to do. The grapevine is also the principal tool used for building consensus, and for testing and generating support for ideas. It can also be used to kill bad ideas and policies before they are written.

USING THE INFORMAL SYSTEM TO LOCATE POWER

A careful study of the formal power system, while historically interesting, will not help the power builder. He or she needs to learn how to use the informal system to find, acquire, and hold on to (maintain) power.

The first requirement is that you have to be plugged into the grapevine. To do that you need to understand what the grapevine really is and how it works. Study the diagram of a grapevine.

The grapevine is a body of information that flows throughout the organization. Everyone working in the company has access to the grapevine. Its use is voluntary. If you understand how the grapevine works, you can become influential through it. If you ignore it, you will face a working life full of surprises, bumps, and starts.

People are not part of the grapevine as individuals but in clusters of four to six people. Hence the name. People are organized into clusters of four to six because that is the size of the average coffee room or cafeteria table. It is also the way most people have been grouped since childhood. Children seated around tables in groups of from four to six is a fairly standard kindergarten room arrangement. The table size is important because most workers trade information over coffee or lunch. Your cluster consists of the group that you associate with regularly.

In small organizations the center of grapevine activity

THE GRAPEVINE

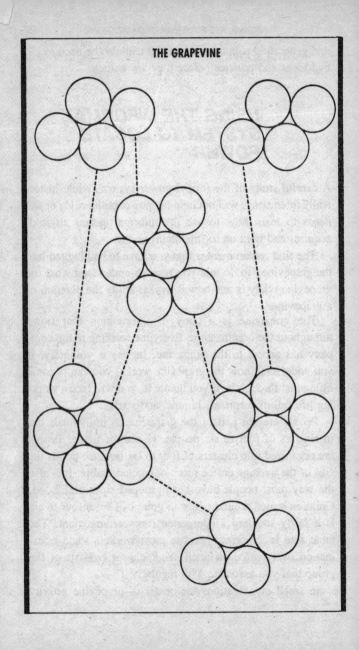

may be the water cooler or the coffeepot on a bookcase shelf. However, the principle is still the same. The people who meet with regularity at either place will form a cluster. Ditto the off-site coffee shop or McDonald's.

Clusters do not form randomly. In order to understand the grapevine, and your relationship to it, you have to see how you came to be in a particular cluster. Think back to your first day at your present job. You will remember that you arrived on time, went to personnel, and filled out W2s and insurance forms. You were then shown to your work station. It could have been a desk in the bullpen, a cubicle, or an office. You were beginning to go through papers on your desk when you realized it was about 10:00 A.M. You did not know this by looking at your watch; you knew this because you could hear people talking as they passed by. They were going for coffee. You had two choices: You could wait until someone asked you to join them, or you could plunge ahead and go to the coffee room alone. If you went alone, you would have to face many strangers by yourself. They would all be looking at you because you were new. You would have to get your coffee and drink it alone or take it back to your desk—an act of cowardice! ("Who is that new guy? He's not very friendly.") You decided to wait. This pattern transcends all levels of the organizational chart. The new vice-president is as likely to hesitate in this situation as the new file clerk.

In a few minutes Gladys, Ethel, and Harry came by and asked if you would like to join them. They were in your department, and you had met them briefly during an interview. You agreed, silently relieved that you would have company. It is a well-known fact that while Americans do not mind sleeping alone, they loathe to eat or drink alone. If you do not believe it, look in a hotel dining room full of business travelers sitting one to a table and watch them bolt their food. The next time you are on an airplane, observe the number of strangers who say nary a word to anyone until the meal is served. When they start eating, they need to talk, and the noise level rises fifty percent.

Your three co-workers were both pleasant and friendly. They immediately began orienting you to the informal system, though they did not actually call it that. They told you about how things really worked. Gladys said that if you needed work processing, you would have to start building a relationship with Jeanette, the department manager. Jeanette was very much a stickler for the rules, but if you got on her good side, she could be persuaded to bend them. Harry said that the boss was going through a trial separation and that any discussion of happy families or faithful wives made him explode. He was also an enthusiastic hockey fan. Ethel told you that she thought the company had had some hard times in the past three years. Its principal product was now obsolete. She had heard from a friend in research that they had made a real breakthough improvement that could sky-rocket the company's stock.

You went back to your work area considerably cheered. Your co-workers seemed friendly and very supportive, and you looked forward to lunch. Again, Gladys, Ethel, and Harry came by for you. At lunch your in-depth education in the ways of the corporate culture and the informal system began. Harry profiled everyone in the department. Gladys gave details about work styles, personal styles, soft spots, and sore spots. It was most helpful. You vowed to keep this information in mind.

The afternoon coffee break was similarly pleasant. You and your co-workers exchanged personal information. You felt remarkably good about your first day specifically and your new job in general. You thought you would like it there. Your boss seemed to believe you could supervise your area. Your supportive co-workers were a pleasant surprise. What could go wrong? You had a good work experience and felt that you would soon be up and running with the new assignment. You left at 5:00 P.M., looking forward to the next day and more of the same.

Unfortunately you got it, and that was the beginning of your troubles. Ethel, Gladys, and Harry came by for you on the second day at 10:00 A.M. and for all subsequent lunches and breaks. Before you even had time to notice it, you were locked into one information group with no way out except "dropping" Harry, Gladys, and Ethel—not a social sin but a political crime! What had happened?

What happened to you happens to approximately ninety-five percent of the people who begin new jobs. Not having been advised to mix with and meet everyone in the office immediately and to keep doing so, you were locked into a cluster on the grapevine before you knew what had happened.

The danger in this occurrence is that you are now locked in with like-minded people. Like-minded people have one important flaw: They agree with you and you with them. What they select to pass on from any other information sources, and everything that they observe, contains only those facts that coincide with their personal world view. You obviously share this view; otherwise you would have found others to eat with on day two of your job. After all, who would choose to eat with someone who gave him indigestion? Sticking with like-minded co-workers is the equivalent of talking to yourself. You hear and assess only a tiny fraction of the total news flowing throughout the organization. None of the news you get—except rumors of an office purge—will challenge your assumptions or shake your relationships. Hence, you will be less powerful. You cannot command the total picture. You will have a lopsided view of what is occurring in the organization. You cannot plan accurately. Your working life is public knowledge. Your alliances are predictable by anyone who is interested enough to look. People watching you could do a formal relationship chart on you, your allies, your enemies, and your relationships within the organization.

What you should have done on day one was go with Harry, Gladys, and Ethel to coffee as you did. At lunch you should have asked someone you did not know to join you, or you could have joined a group of strangers. You should have talked with as many people from as many different departments as possible. As a new employee your behavior would not have startled anyone particularly or have aroused suspicion. It would even have been viewed with approval. "Here is someone who is trying to meet everyone. He wants to be friendly." There would have been no question of hurting the three musketeers. You did not know them well enough to dislike them, nor would they have assumed that you did. You were simply trying to meet all of your new co-workers. You would have laid the foundation for power building.

Look at your own office situation. Are you eating and drinking with the same people every day, oblivious to the fact that you have cut yourself off from vast quantities of information? If you have let this happen (you're not alone if you have) and you really care about power, you're going to have to reorganize your office social relationships. You have seen only the tip of the iceberg. You cannot acquire information or build relationships until you gain access to the majority of the information clusters and their leaders in your company. The only way to do this is to spend less time with your closest networking group.

There is a potential political problem here. If you abruptly decide to leave your comrades of long standing, the janitor may find your still warm body tucked under the steam table in the lunchroom. You have to continue to see your primary group regularly. Once or twice a week you can vary the time you eat or drink so that you can join another group.

This is easy to do if you understand what is likely to happen when you join a group of strangers. They will look up. If you don't know them or they you, introductions are in order. You say, "May I join you?" They say, "Sure." You do. They continue their conversation while you listen and possibly make a remark or two. Unless someone is describing his or her sex life in detail or trading salary information, the group will be only momentarily curious about your presence. After all, they do not own the cafeteria table. The space is available to anyone.

Think about the grapevine again. If all this is true, then how do people in so many separate groups share information? To be more powerful you would have to become a cross-pollinator or meet others who were. Cross-pollinators are influential people who share information and move randomly from group to group. In a company with three thousand people there would be ten to twenty cross-pollinators. You must identify and cultivate these people. They are the ones who spread the impressions and reactions to the news of many different clusters. They are infinitely more powerful than those who simply react because they have done more research and have built broader relationships. As a result of their power they also incur more risk.

If you became a cross-pollinator, some people who had never noticed you before would begin to see you differently.

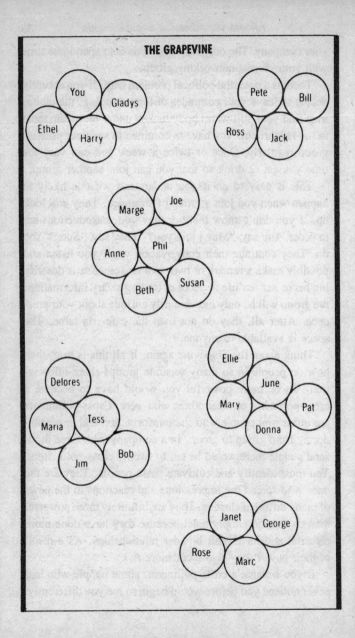

THE GRAPEVINE

Your boss would probably begin picking your brain. The risk inherent in this is that although you would appear to be more knowledgeable to your boss, you would also appear less manageable. Never again would you be surprised by something that happened within the organization. You would clearly see that there are no corporate secrets, only news that you have not heard because you lacked ears in the right place.

The cornerstone of the power building process is the total internal information network. Information is a power component everywhere, and you need many sources of it. You need to look for a particular kind of information. What you have to research in your personal quest for power is the kind of power your bosses, peers, and even your subordinates have. Until you know what you are up against you cannot build a power base or, as we will explain later, do surgery on anyone else's.

RESEARCHING POWER

In order to research power we need to divide it into four categories—position power, personal power, alliance power, and financial power.

1. *Position power* is the most common form of power in the organization. It is tacitly accepted by most people, and it is highly visible. Position power is the power inherent solely in a person's position in the hierarchy. For instance, even if the CEO in your company is weak beyond comprehension, he is still entitled to a certain protocol. People will not publicly point out that he is consulted only as a courtesy and not because his opinion is valued, considered, or even necessary to a particular decision.

Position power may include the perks of high office without any basis. For instance, the sales manager may, in fact, report to his three- or four-star salespeople. Even though he still has an unlimited expense account and a new Buick every year, he cannot order them to do everything. The university president may be without any policy-making power, even though he presides at graduation exercises and alumni events, and welcomes the victorious football team back to town as its lead supporter.

Position power was far more common in the 1970s because companies had more paternalistic attitudes then. If good old George, the president of the company, was circumvented more often than he was consulted, it was because times were good and there was no need to force a confrontation. The company was profitable, so why rock the boat? What did it matter that George had not made a significant contribution or decision in ten years? He was a good guy. In the 1980s only the richest companies can afford Georges. Most will ruthlessly prune such people, some by firing, others by forcibly retiring them.

One of the common management myths is that CEOs can act entirely independent of subordinates. This is rarely true, even in owner/founder or family-owned businesses. Most CEOs must sell their subordinates on the wisdom of a particular action rather than promulgate it. If they impose rather than sell and the decision turns out to be a mistake, the CEO's job will be at risk and he or she will be all alone, literally left holding the bag.

Most CEOs approve rather than design. It would be fatal for a CEO to ingore the marketing manager's input on a final marketing plan when the CEO did not create the plan. Since he does not know the history of the plan, he will incur great risk if he does more than fine-tune it. The same is true of financial plans. Life at the top tends to be collaborative.

Position power may mean that, although the person is deferred to and consulted formally, his or her advice is never seriously sought out or valued. There is a major difference. Many CEOs and other top management people only realized how little power they actually had when they began to analyze whose opinions became the basis of policy. They were consulted only because it violated the formal system if they were not. Decisions were still made through the informal system.

2. *Personal power* is a kind of corporate charisma. Certain people are personally well liked and have a special influence. The company handyman, who may not even be on the formal chart, is cultivated by power builders throughout the company. He has personal power for many reasons: He sees much more of the total picture because he hears more and talks to a wider audience. He has a certain charm, and people like him; they ignore the fact that he lacks position power. He is a barometer of people's moods and expectations, and he has a certain shrewdness and detachment which make him an acute observer.

A senior secretary in the same company, independent of her boss, is always consulted about personnel policies by the personnel department. She has a facility for anticipating how other people in the company—at all levels, not just her own—will react. She has been right so often that the personnel director consults her as a matter of course. She has carved out this power niche for herself.

The head of the data processing department has made himself disagreeable to so many people by speaking BASIC instead of English that people move around him. A subordinate is consulted on major decisions; the boss is then informed of what others have already decided. The boss may have the title, but he has so little influence that people feel quite free to ignore him. He has abdicated as manager and continues as resident critic—not a highly sought-after or powerful role.

Personal power is the most difficult kind to pinpoint because we are trained to look for power only above us on the corporate ladder. The underlying assumption in most corporate relationships is that two things occur as you move up the organization chart: Those moving up tend to be older, and age inevitably brings the wisdom of experience and training. If only this were true! Unfortunately, it is entirely possible for people without good qualities to be promoted, solely because they are inoffensive and satisfied to get the title.

You can identify people with personal power only if you cultivate detachment. You have to be able to see objectively who listens to whom, regardless of their relative positions. Certainly those subordinates who greatly influence their bosses tend to have considerable personal power, often more power than their bosses. That explains why personal power occurs everywhere in an organization. It is also the reason why people in high places do not necessarily have power.

Personal power is always deliberate. It comes into play because someone who possesses it says, "I can help with that" or "Here's what I think may happen." Hospital nurses often have enormous personal power with doctors. They advise and update the doctor based on their research, insights, and very different perspectives. People who choose to build a power base solely on personal influence tend to be very similar to the political operative in government. They value power because it makes them feel that they have the ability to control events. Such people may enjoy what they have but may not necessarily aspire to expand their influence. An exception to this occurs when someone uncovers an issue that he or she feels passionately about and begins to use personal power to further this issue.

The hallmark of personal power is influence, and if someone is powerful, he or she will use this influence routinely. People who have personal power use that power in a variety of helpful or detrimental ways. Their own interests do not have to be threatened for them to act. Keep this in mind when you are trying to discover how much power a person really has. For instance, a powerful secretary may help some salesmen get appointments ahead of others with her boss. She can quash a new personnel department ability test through the grapevine. She may even dissuade a co-worker from initiating an act of revenge directed against a third person.

3. *Alliance power* is power based on numbers. Eight people getting together for coffee or lunch to have earnest discussions are forming alliances. They are either against something (about sixty-five percent of the time) or for something. They unite because they believe that management will give more consideration to a decision if it knows it faces a phalanx of organized opposition or support.

Alliances vary in size from two to a multitude. There are always alliances in flux. All alliances are shaky, for unless all parties work for the same boss, anyone in the alliance can be detached at will by his/her boss. An alliance of three is the most unstable because it has the potential to end up as two against one, with each of the three taking a turn at being the "one." Alliances are always extremely visible, and the results of their influence is easy to track. Remember that eight people having coffee together (or any group larger than six) violates the natural order. They stand out.

Alliances require considerable maintenance. Keeping all of the members of a group equally happy requires time, energy, and a leader. The person trying to keep the group together would have a difficult time getting his or her own work done.

From a power building perspective mapping alliances is very important. The most important thing to know is what the basis of the alliance is. If all of the secretaries in the department unite to keep any one of them from having to make coffee, it is an issue alliance. If three secretaries and two salespeople fight a boss they dislike, it is a political alliance. If six malcontents feel their division is being mismanaged (but not by their immediate boss), it may be an assassination committee.

4. *Money or financial power* is the fourth kind of organizational power. Because financial resources are limited, money is an important source of contention and power. If more money is budgeted for the marketing department, then production may be asked to make budget cuts. If research and development can influence organizational opinion and reach top management, both formally and informally, they will measure success by budget increases.

Within a department, budgets are even more of an object of power struggles. It is not just the division of the salary pie that produces the problem, although people can always be expected to struggle over raises. The overall budget, and particularly its individual allocations, causes the most problems.

In many companies a manager will delegate the preparation of the annual budget to a subordinate and specify certain guidelines. Within those guidelines the subordinate is free to allocate funds. When this occurs money power will immediately shift away from the manager to the subordinate. Others in the department will now bring their arguments to the subordinate, even though he or she has only been delegated to act in this instance. If someone is dissatisfied, he or she can still go to the boss and complain. The manager could then appear to "overrule" his subordinate, giving the impression that he definitely has the complainer's interest at heart. By delegating the budget preparation, the manager in effect says to the department, "This isn't really important. Look, I'm not making the decisions myself." Nobody is fooled, of course. After all, if money isn't important to an organization, what is?

Money games are also played at the next level up. Infinite numbers of people have spent thousands of man-hours preparing budget statements only to learn that they have participated in an exercise in futility. The decisions were already made before the budgets were due. The time they spent preparing these statements was supposed to give them a feeling of participation without relinquishing any power. When this happens, employees fight back by using the old budget, retyped, forever after. They may also ignore the new budget entirely, spend whatever is needed, and leave the boss to fend for himself when the internal auditor calls.

Money power may reside not in the person who approves the budget but with whoever signs the requisitions. The person who must sign individual requests or audit the budget can influence the expenditures tremendously by simply putting through or detaining requests. An accounting clerk can have significant power simply as a gatekeeper in the financial process.

Furthermore, money is concrete. It has a cachet which makes it important as a symbol. A department with a larger budget will always seem more important than one whose budget is much smaller, even if the latter's work is more important overall. Power builders must reckon with the symbolic value of money as well as with the actual numbers.

Once you have identified the sources of power in your own area, you will need to analyze that information in an organizational context. To do that you will need to look at your professional and personal styles.

3. WHAT IS YOUR PROFESSIONAL/ PERSONAL STYLE?

DAVID McMartin believed himself a very tough-minded, take-charge guy. After ten years with the same automobile parts manufacturing firm, he felt accepted; his self-image meshed nicely with the company's style. Imagine his surprise and bewilderment when the company retained a psychologist to give personality and psychological tests to managers to enable them to adapt to what it saw as changing conditions. David thought the tests foolish—but worse was the psychologist's recommendation that he not be promoted to a higher level because of his "difficulty in getting along with others." The report went on to conclude that "McMartin lacks sensitivity to others such that any productivity programs he participates in are likely to fail." Somehow David's style was no longer acceptable.

There are fashions in personal styles just as there are current trends in clothing, interior decorating, and the arts. If you were growing up in or have read much about the

1960s, you will know that the rallying cry of that era was "Do your own thing." The 1970s modified this cry to "Do your own thing if it improves you." The self-improvement craze is not yet over, but some of the enthusiasm has certainly dimmed. Today's uncertain economy, though not as depressed as in the first few years of this decade, keeps people from becoming totally absorbed in perfecting themselves. The evolving theme for the 1980s seems to be, "Submerge your individuality. Do what works."

Individualism is not now, and probably never has been, a truly popular theme in organizations. The past is often hard to judge because we have records only of what people said, not what they thought. The whole productivity movement of the 1980s, especially quality circles, can be thought of as an effort to blend people and to build teams, not to identify and cultivate high achievers.

Today's economic climate certainly does not encourage new businesses. It is extremely difficult to launch a new business, as capital is both scarce and costly. However, corporate caution and rising cost cuts have made the formation of many new businesses inevitable. Corporations have so ruthlessly held in their freewheelers that many have left to form their own businesses. Companies are beginning to feel a creativity drain as self-employment becomes fashionable among high achievers. Some companies have begun to fight this exodus by restructuring to encourage the entrepreneurial type to stay with the company as head of a new sub unit.

What does this mean to you? First, if you have previously made assumptions about the "best" style for acquiring power, then you need to test those assumptions. You may be caught in a time warp. What motivated people in the 1960s does not necessarily work in the 1980s. The economic climate is not the only difference: individual values are changing as well. While you are busy planning to acquire power, you are under observation by those above, next to, and below you. What do they see? If you could stand outside yourself and look at the total you, especially your professional and personal style, what impression would you form? Self-analysis is critical to power building. Unless you know how others perceive and interpret what you do, you cannot make valid power-building decisions. You will always be doing the wrong thing based on faulty logic or, if you do make the right decision, you will not understand why it was right and therefore will be unable to duplicate it.

As you analyze both your work style and your personal style, you are going to be making important decisions. You will be comparing your personal style with styles that work now. It is not a question of whether you can adjust to a current fad. That is "old think" from the 1970s. You are not infinitely adaptable. Your choice will be whether you can and are willing to change your style if you discover that your current style is not helpful to power building. You will be deciding whether you should change your work theater to one which values your style. To begin this process you need to determine exactly what your style is.

If you divided work into two main parts, you would have "what" and "how" elements. The what elements are the skills you use on the job and your output. Style is the how element in everything. How do you live? How do you approach work? How do you actually perform your job?

As you analyze "style" you should also analyze your image. Image is the total result, personal and professional, that other people see, while style is the approach you use to do your job. Although you may have absolute control over both your style and image, you still cannot ignore others' assumptions. For instance, John Deveraux, a systems engineer, thought of himself as a high-energy person. He felt that he appeared to vibrate with energy early in the morning. Contrary to John's idea, his colleagues believed that either he had terminal coffee nerves or had stuck his finger in an electrical outlet. This dichotomy of perception is very common when someone is consciously trying to create a personal image that is not second nature.

How people see you affects how they behave toward you and, most important, the kinds of relationships they will form with you. To yourself you may be as lovable as Dickens's Tiny Tim—but your co-workers may see you as Ebenezer Scrooge. You cannot see yourself realistically (much less make changes) unless you have some sense of how you come across to others. You do not need to ask people what they think, a look at how they react to you can be very revealing.

John Molloy, the author of *Dress for Success*, demonstrated this in his book. He pointed out that those who wear beige raincoats appear to be more successful to more people than those who wear black, brown, or navy raincoats, including to the people actually wearing dark-colored raincoats! The person who wears a black raincoat may actually be more successful than someone who hocked his grandmother's silver to buy a Burberry, but no one will recognize or acknowledge this fact on sight. Although his image may be at odds with the facts, most people will respond first to the image he projects.

It does not matter whether you are a supervisor or a senior vice-president, you have a distinctive work style. We are going to look at style as it affects power within the organization from two points of view: (1) What is your working style for getting results, building and maintaining relationships, and defining and holding territory; and (2) What is your personal (nonwork) style? It is easiest to analyze your work style by looking at your approach to problems. In order to determine your style in results and relationships, ask yourself the following questions.

RELATIONSHIP STYLES

1. Are you project-oriented or is yours a "tending" or "maintenance" style? Please don't overreact to the word "maintenance"; it has no built-in negative qualities. Many responsible jobs require a "tending" style. Knowing and understanding how you approach an assignment will give you useful clues as to what your style is. This is especially important in determining if there is a match of styles with your boss and the overall organization.

Suppose you are told that an important presentation to top management must be made three weeks from today. You need to see that information is gathered and organized, and a script written or at least well thought out. Graphics need to be prepared, rehearsals scheduled, and space and coffee service planned for. A time must be set for the presentation and the participants notified.

How do you approach this assignment? If you are project-oriented, you will not think of this assignment as part of your ordinary work but as a special project. You will approach it as a one-time shot, giving it all you've got. If you are a "tender," you may think, "This kind of assignment is probably going to be called for again. I should try to develop methods that will make it easier the next time."

A project-oriented style means that you arc over the work to the result. You do not particularly care about method or whether you will learn anything as long as it is a success. The project-oriented manager is attracted by newness. The "tender" might see this project as an opportunity to train a subordinate, experiment with a new method, or test a policy developed during the last emergency. Of course the "tender" wants results, but he or she is equally interested in how this project fits into or departs from departmental methods.

You may find that while your style changes somewhat situationally, one style usually tends to dominate over time.

2. What is your relationship style? How do you work with and through others? Here are some of the most common relationship styles ranked from most to least useful.

EFFECTIVE STYLES

Consensus Style. Yours is a consensus style if you are more comfortable blending many ideas into a generalized concept that everyone will support instead of imposing your own ideas on the group. You reject superstars and tangents, and you will not implement a decision until you are sure that all objections have been answered and everyone is ready to accept the decision. You expect to lead or persuade everyone to make a commitment to the solution. For example, your department is going to buy new desks. Half of the people favor wooden desks, and the rest want painted steel. You want to get the group to reach a mutually satisfactory decision. It takes twelve hours of meetings, about ninety minutes at a stretch, to reach a decision that satisfies everyone. A consensus-style manager would not think twice about the amount of time it took to reach this decision. Managers with different styles would have imposed their ideas much earlier.

Consensus-style management is said to be part of the Japanese success story as workers buy in to company goals. Many American managers believe consensus building is the Japanese revenge for Hiroshima and Nagasaki. How much do you use the input of others when you have both the responsibility for a decision and the power to dictate? If consensus seems tedious and cumbersome to you, it is not your best style! Consensus-style management is very fashionable right now as more organizations try to involve employees in the decision-making process in order to increase worker commitment, output, and work quality.

Manipulative-Consensus. There is a substyle here which might be called manipulative-consensus. A manager with this style asks everyone in a particular area what he or she thinks should be done, and what each would like to do. The manager may collect all the voices, but he or she alone will make the decision. The manager operates under a facade of consensus, but in the end does exactly what he or she wanted to do in the first place. The difference is that his subordinates think they had a say in the final decision.

Sales Style. Yours is a sales style if your approach is to try to sell your boss, co-workers, or subordinates on whatever you want done or on whatever action you want them to take. If no one reports to you, you will try to sell others on the benefits of helping you. You do not try to elicit guilt in order to convince others to do things your way. If you cannot sell your ideas to others, you will see it as your lack of skill, not their perversity.

For instance, when your secretary says that she feels an inner conflict when she is doing your Christmas shopping on company time, you do not take it as insubordination or as a personal threat to your power. You simply redouble your effort to convince her that she is an indispensable part of the team and that what you have asked her to do helps the team.

Your approach to most problems is "What is in it for them?" You are rarely troubled by issues of "fairness" and "rightness." You are often haunted by a fear that your co-workers are not totally committed. You use this style with family and friends, too.

This is a timeless style because it is honestly more involving for more people and thus tends to reduce conflict. The manager's skill at selling ideas is critical. Some people are unable to use this style because they lack an understanding of basic selling skills and compound the problem by refusing to learn them.

Decisive Style. This comes across as a high-energy style. If you are more interested in making a decision than in the contemplation of possible alternatives, you may fit here. It is a lower risk style than you might assume. Even if you do make the wrong decision, if it is made immediately there will still be time to make changes. For instance, if you begin a project immediately, even if you do not have a completed plan, you can always readjust later. Even if you have charged off in the wrong direction, there's time to redirect. This style is more flamboyant, and it suggests someone who is in charge. It is also useful in business where rapid change is now a permanent part of the environment.

Decisive people put little emotional burden on those they work with. If someone makes a mistake, the boss says, "Let's try this next." Contrast that with the indecisive style that says, "We must think of something!" More managers are now trying to use a decisive style because it reassures everyone who is watching, especially superiors. It also motivates subordinates.

Political Style. The political style is a high-risk, high-reward, very pragmatic style. Perceptions, rather than wins and losses, are what count. If someone has a political style, he or she analyzes all work from the perspective "What will be the effect on my career and/or boss if what I'm doing doesn't work out?"

A political style does not focus on the immediate effect but on implications and long-term effects. A project that fails anonymously is almost as good as a success because there is no long-term harm to the politician from the failure. "Results first" is not always the political attitude. If your style is political, and your boss really likes a co-worker who is minimally competent, you would not point out your co-worker's shortcomings to your boss unless this co-worker directly threatens your place. If a boss requires regular ego feeding, you will provide it. The political style is always concerned with either upward mobility or with the protection of territory or prerogatives.

Jack Martin worked for an advertising agency as an account executive when the agency got a new computer system. Jack feared, quite correctly, that he would now be more dependent on the data processing people for information. He learned the access codes and procedures so he could get needed information without working through the data processing department.

Jack perceived that rather than be left to the mercy of the data processing staff, access to the computer system could be used as a power lever to increase his power. The political style is probably the oldest and most widely recognized one. It undoubtedly comes from the military and espouses the philosophy of do not upset your superiors and incidentally win the war. This style, if used properly, will always get good results.

LESS EFFECTIVE STYLES

Manipulative Style. A manipulator believes that selling people is entirely too much trouble. He or she not only does not have a clue as to how subordinates feel about work decisions but does not really care. Manipulators believe that people must be forcibly motivated. They talk about "happy families," "teams," and "friendships," but what manipulators really want is for people to do what the manipulator wants them to do. The manipulator will insinuate, suggest, attempt to raise guilt, and use other quasi-emotional approaches to get people to act as he or she desires. Manipulators see no harm in this style, nor do their subordinates or peers object to it; all of them feel free to use the same tactics. They achieve the desired results, and that is what counts.

The boss needs people to work during the Memorial Day weekend. At a staff meeting she says, "We must get ahead on the project next weekend. I was planning to take my children to the shore, but now I'll have to stay in the city because of the workload." The talk focuses on all that she's giving up until a subordinate jumps in and agrees to help. Men use this style more often than women, but the women who do use it are often better at it. There is no older style; it is positively biblical!

The greatest danger inherent in this style is that manipulators sometimes forget that their actions are deliberate. If they eventually try to change to a more adult-to-adult style, they will confuse people who will not understand the switch. Manipulative style is much criticized and could hardly be said to be in vogue. Still, it is widely used and, if well done, even admired.

Social Worker Style. A social-worker-style manager wants people to be happy (or at least content) almost as much as he/she wants them to get the work out. If you use the social worker style, you are frequently frustrated and regularly disappointed by the methods and attitudes your co-workers and subordinates display. You care whether people want to do a particular job because you see a direct link between feelings and results. You often blame yourself, when events don't progress as planned, for not having explained things properly.

One can easily identify a social worker by looking at the performance appraisals he or she completes. A social worker will always insert comments on attitude and sincerity (as he/she detects them) in the written appraisal. He or she will measure achievement by commitment and sincerity and will always downgrade someone who does not exhibit these qualities. Social workers are often labeled "touchy/feely" types because their attitude toward their subordinates says, "I want you to want to do the job my way. If you don't, please behave as if you do. In other words, give a performance. Convince me."

The social worker style is a hallmark of nonprofit organizations. Universities love to talk about the sincerity of individual faculty people during tenure hearings, even though there is no relationship between scholarly or classroom competence and sincerity. This style was fashionable in the 1960s because society at large believed sincerity equaled results. It is still fashionable with people caught in a 1960s time warp. This style strikes many top management people as soft. Does sincerity really improve results or would the hypocritical but effective produce even better results?

Command Style. The quasi-military command style is still the most universal. It is especially widespread in heavy manufacturing, parts of the health care industry, some public relations departments, and pockets of banking and accounting, but do not think it is only there. Commanders turn up in neighborhood drug stores, restaurants, and day-care centers. Many people adopt this style to some extent during recessions, reorganizations, and crises of confidence. Even though it can be bad for business, command is reassuring both to the user and the recipient because it says, "I am assigned to do this job; obviously I must know how to do it." It also enables people not to think critically about what they are doing. It is easier to jump in and do the job. Commanders—and even commandos—frequently have very loyal subordinates because they provide a strong, almost parental sense of security. Relieved by their commander of the responsibility to make judgments, they do only as told and only as much as required. It takes commanders a long time to recognize this problem. Some never do.

The command style is a very explosive style for power builders because it creates free-floating opposition groups. This style tends to polarize people, as commanders know no middle ground. Everyone who works with or for them is on one end or the other of the continuum. Because there is no middle ground, the people who refuse to go along with a commander either leave or are eventually fired.

The command style is undergoing a revival of interest as the consensus style begins to come under fire. This style should be embraced with caution because in pure form it is a very high-risk management style. It can be very successful, but if it fails, no one feels obliged to rescue the commander from his or her follies. Subordinates who were the most eager and willing to let their superiors dictate policies to them will be the first ones to deny any personal responsibility when those policies fail.

Fire Fighter Style. A fire fighter style results from a combination of boredom and procrastination. A great many people hate decision making. As a result they usually wind up making crisis decisions. The attraction of this style is that it is more exciting to make routine decisions at the last minute than day to day. The duller the job, the more likely a person is to slip into a fire fighter mentality. Fire fighting causes few problems if the issues to be resolved are minor. It is disastrous, however, if policy decisions have to be made. It often looks like the decisive style but is really shooting from the hip.

Fire fighting is essentially a kind of gambling. The higher the fire fighter is in the organization, the greater the potential damage. It is extremely common in start-up companies and accounts for many failures. For example, the new company needs a controller to organize its financial area. Two bookkeepers are presently handling all of the accounting. Top management considers the entire area tedious and, with the exception of the profit/loss statements, unimportant. A firefighter manager will not hire a controller unless the IRS calls to schedule an audit, leaving everyone in panic and the new employee under the gun.

Legal Style. A legal style follows policy and procedures precisely and attracts people who want and need safety. The perceived safety in rules is ill-founded; there is none. Only an illusion of safety exists. These people believe strongly that if policy is honored, results should follow. "All bases are covered. Nobody can say we didn't follow the rules" is the rallying cry of the legalistic manager. Personnel departments often take the same stance when they look for the lowest-risk candidates. If a project or employee fails, this procedure provides personnel with both a reason and an excuse. There are many companies—some of which actually make a profit—where rules are revered and the revision of these rules is considered a productive, full-time job. If personnel is very influential, rather than a high-turnover catchall, the power structure values a legalistic style. You will not be surprised to learn that lawyers who get into management are not "born again" into a different management style. Most retain a legalistic outlook.

One of the funniest recent examples of the limitations of a legal style is the policy of many banks forbidding married couples, or close relatives, from working for the same bank. It is perfectly acceptable for two commercial banking officers to live together; only marriage is prohibited. This utterly defeats the intent of the policy, which was designed to prevent workers from conspiring to defraud or control the bank or any of its departments. The legalists cannot actually tell these employees they cannot live together; how would that look in the company policy manual? It is left to the political types to discipline through the informal system. This is only one weakness of a legal style. Being able to deal directly with embryonic problems is vital to good management. When only the concrete can be reworked it is often too late to do so. The heavy dependency on policy encourages inflexibility.

Tight Style. Tight is a variation of the legal style. A person with a tight style tends to keep information, resources, and decisions under control. If you have a tight style, you know precisely whom you owe and who owes you. You might not actually keep score in writing, but then again you might. You are interested in keeping things boxed up. You like the idea that your subordinates are just a little bit nervous when you are around. Some people refer to this style as "anal retentive." It is commonest in creative areas with people who think of the job and work environment as living theater.

Abdication Style. A "no-fault" style basically lets people do what they want to do as long as they get results or at least something approximating results. An abdicating manager does not lead or direct; he or she simply sees to it that accidents that could threaten his or her career do not occur. This is a very popular style in nonprofit organizations, especially universities.

If the department chairman lets the faculty "work it out," then they will be forced to deal with the problem, and the chairman won't have to be bothered. What actually happens in these situations is that departmental secretaries grab power. Students quickly learn that the last person to see with a problem is the dean or department chairman. Looked at from outside this style seems very territorial. People who really do not want to manage will still retaliate against anyone who tries to nip off a piece of territory.

This style is an attempt to reduce risk while the user awaits developments. It is disastrous in swiftly changing situations because the drifting often results in reduced options when a decision must finally be made. It also means people are frequently defending something that has already disappeared.

It has been possible in universities only because the environment was unhurried and relatively secure. Until now there was no real need to get commitment from the rank and file or take the risks of making firm decisions. These conditions no longer exist. As student populations continue to shrink, the vital decisions about how universities are to be run will require deans who can make decisions, take risks, and otherwise manage.

Secretive Style. Whispered conversations, veiled glances at the water cooler, and thirty people trying to occupy a ten-stall washroom are rarely necessary; they are simply outcroppings of a particular management style. The closed door and secret meetings say, "I am controlling power by controlling information; I can keep people from knowing." This is not true, of course. As you know from chapter two, information is widely available to anyone with the determination and energy to gather it. However, the effect of this style is to make others think that they are either in on, or excluded from, something "really important." The secretive style is polarizing within a work group, but it can increase the user's power during periods of company instability. If people begin to believe that the secretive person does not really know more, his or her power will evaporate. As a result, many secretive managers spend long hours seeking information.

In many service businesses top management has difficulty explaining the logic of certain decisions because none exists. The logic is simply someone's gut-level feelings. The real reason may be politically unpalatable: The client wants it that way, no matter what. A secretive style lends such behavior drama until the underlying vacuum is uncovered.

Conditional Style. This style might be characterized by the words "either/or." Either someone will do something or someone will not. If the person with this style has some political skill, he or she can create an impression of calm rationality. If not, he or she will seem indecisive. There is a significant difference. The conditional style does not indicate a fear of making decisions; it implies the desire to balance alternatives. Although it is similar to the abdication style, the conditional manager will make a decision if he or she must. The main weakness of this approach is that the manager's need to balance alternatives often distorts the information. What if there are not an equal number of equally attractive alternatives? Lots of energy can be consumed looking for them or, in extreme cases, manufacturing them.

The conditional style often occurs because top management favors a command style for which conditional is a perfect foil. By choosing between equal alternatives—no matter how the facts were tortured to produce this equality—the commander seems more reasonable and less arbitrary.

A summary of the way these styles occur in various industries appears on pages 60–61. You will see patterns within industries that are a result of the attraction such businesses have for certain personality types. This chart's greatest value to you may be as an early warning that you have chosen an industry or an area where your management style and the industry's traditonal style diverge. For instance, if yours is a command style, you will be miserable in a university deanship. You will also, within minutes of appointment, be a political outcast. A consensus or political style could help you become president of the university.

ANALYZING YOUR PERSONAL STYLE

Relationships not only affect power building but are also crucial to work satisfaction. A conflict in personal style with a co-worker or several co-workers can reduce your effectiveness and your job satisfaction to zero. How does your

INDUSTRIES IN WHICH IT IS USEFUL

MANAGEMENT STYLE	Accounting Investment Banking Consulting	Banking Insurance Financial Consulting	Health Care	Nonprofit	Manufacturing	Glamour Industries	Self-employment	Prospects for 1980s
THE GOOD								
Consensus	Will be tried in staff areas	Will be tried in staff areas	Will be used with staff and non-MD medical staff	Not widespread before 1985	Already being tried in about 20% of companies	Not applicable; tried and abandoned in some companies	Not applicable	A fad which disturbs middle management power building
Manipulative-Consensus	Pockets in middle management	Top management uses occasionally	Widespread	Widespread	Seen as too much trouble	Very widespread	Too much trouble for many	Pockets in almost every industry. If well done, it can be effective short-term
Sales	Growing with people under 40	Undergoing critical review	Rare	Rare	Rare	Used by those who are not political	Thought to be better outside the company	Comes and goes; more widespread in good economic times
Decisive	Not widely used	Not widely used	Not widely used	Not understood; alien to culture	Getting stronger here	Rare	Increasing	Growing in popularity

Political	Most used by top management	Most used by top management	Used in pockets	Not well understood nor widely used	Used widely in Fortune "500"	Always	Not widely used	Very durable style, timeless, pragmatic
THE BAD								
Manipulative	Used by top management	Used by some managers	Common	Very common	Too much trouble	Very common	Very common	Reduces productivity
Social Worker	Rare	Rare	Widespread	Widespread	Rare	Rare	Rare	Requires a mindset most often found in nonprofit
Command	Widely used	Widely used	Rare, but pockets	Only MDs use it	Still a dominant style	Pockets	Widely used	Antiproductivity but will diminish slowly because it is fun
Fire Fighter	Used by staff people and support	Used by staff people and support	Rare	Rare	Widespread	Used by staff	Widely used	Will always be used if people are underworked
Legal	Top management still favors	Top management still favors	Widely used	Widely used	Used in high-tech businesses	Rare	Rare	Troubled companies only

| | INDUSTRIES IN WHICH IT IS USEFUL | | | | | | | |
MANAGE-MENT STYLE	Accounting Investment Banking Consulting	Banking Insurance Financial Consulting	Health Care	Nonprofit	Manufacturing	Glamour Industries	Self-employment	Prospects for 1980s
THE OFF-THE-WALL								
Abdication/Weak	In "old line" firms	Dying out	Common	Favored by academics	Rare	Rare	Very rare	Dying out except in companies so troubled there is no hope
Secretive	Sign of powerlessness	Not what it was	Overworked	Common	Rare	Game players	Very rare	Pockets in troubled companies
Conditional	Rare	Rare	Common	Very common	Very rare	Very rare	Very rare	Dying out

personal style affect your professional style? How can it help or hurt you as you build and maintain relationships? People's expectations about organizational style and the styles of co-workers are vital to both productivity and job satisfaction. For instance, in talking with literally hundreds of job hunters about why they voluntarily left jobs before securing others, the reason most often given was enforced sociability, that is, the pressure to be with co-workers in a nonwork setting on their own time.

You might have expected work load, management style, office politics, or salary grievances to be major considerations, especially since most people loathe and fear job hunting. Although these variables were important, none compared with forced after-work socializing. This was true even when people said that they actually liked their co-workers as individuals. Your feelings on this issue will color all your power-building decisions, even if you have never consciously thought about it. After all, people generally change jobs for rational reasons; for example, "It's good for my career." "It's fifteen percent more money than I'm getting now." "I'm bored and the company's shaky." These reasons will never prevent job dissatisfaction if the personal styles of co-workers are not compatible or if the pressure to socialize exists. To prevent such problems you need to know your personal style.

1. Groupie versus loner. Put yourself on a continuum from extremely outgoing to hermit. Where would you fit? Ask yourself the following questions and answer according to your behavior in the office and/or with your co-workers.

A. Do you find someone to have coffee with if your regular cronies are not available? Are you just as happy to bring a cup of coffee back to your desk and continue your work? ✓

B. Do you initiate an after-work drink with a co-worker, especially when you do not particularly like the person and are not interested in drinking anyway? Do you see this kind of socializing as a necessary evil? ✓

C. Of the going-away parties, showers, and general celebrations held in your office last year, how many did you attend? More than half? Of those you did attend, did you stay for more than half of the event? ✓

D. Do you schedule errands at lunch or immediately after work to avoid socializing with co-workers?

E. Do you know the names of your co-workers' spouses or lovers? ✓

F. During the work day do you spend any time engaged in purely personal (nonjob-related) gossip? (If two co-workers are having an affair, that is office as well as personal gossip. See the chapter on sex in the office.)

G. Do you feel the need to spend time with co-workers? Has your boss alluded to your "being a team player"? ✗

H. Do you entertain co-workers in your home? Was this because you wanted to or because you felt that it was politically necessary? ✓

If you have ever thought of changing jobs because the atmosphere in your organization was too social or not social enough, you will want to look at this section carefully. Your work relationships are critical if you are going to become deeply involved in power building. You cannot be a long-term success if you and your co-workers have radically different needs and expectations. The issue here is not whether you can meet expectations; you can and must, if you care about your career.

What you are trying to decipher from your answers to these questions is how much time you spend with co-workers and how agreeable it is to you. It is a misnomer to call any of these get-togethers "social" events for it is impossible to have a truly social, that is, personal, relationship with people that you work with and for. Too much is at stake politically. All of these get-togethers are essentially off-site business meetings, and most people, however reluctantly, treat socializing as part of the job to be done.

If most of your answers were yes, with the exception of D, then you tend to be a groupie. People build closer working relationships with those who are like-minded and who have similar styles. The trust dimension in office relationships, that is, how much people can and do trust each other, however, depends on similarities in style every time. It is more difficult for people to trust someone whose behavior tends to be unpredictable or inexplicable.

There are no preferred answers to these questions. What you want to get from your answers is a sense of where you are within the organization so that, after we analyze the corporate culture in the next chapter, you will be able to see if there is a match. A groupie in one place might blend in with the landscape. In another company he or she would be thought of as pathetically insecure. "Good heavens," co-workers say, "can't he or she do anything alone?"

2. People- or problem-oriented. Even if your answers to the questions in section one indicated that you were a loner,

you may still have some people-oriented tendencies. A people-oriented style means that you are inclined to think of the effects of a decision, a remark, or a change in policy in terms of specific people or a particular type of person. For instance, suppose you have to decide whether to authorize the purchase for the typing pool of green-screened or black-and-white-screened computer display terminals. If you are problem-oriented, your first question will be whether green or black-and-white displays are cheaper and more durable. If you are people-oriented, your first concern will be the effects of this decision on the people in the department. It is a matter of gut-level response. React positively or negatively to the following statements.

A. Policy decisions should always serve the bottom line before the needs of individuals are considered. The company's survival and profit/loss come first.

B. When I am making a decision, I generally think first about costs.

C. In the past year I have made several management or peer decisions because I did not want someone to leave or become upset, or to cause trouble within the department.

D. Giving in can be a useful strategy especially when the issue is trivial.

Once again, there are no correct or incorrect answers. Your goal here is to determine your orientation toward decision making. If you responded negatively to A and B and positively to letters C and D, then you tend to be people-oriented. A positive response to A and B indicates that you tend to be problem-oriented.

In many companies a people-oriented style is at odds with the need to increase output. In others, the strict problem approach lowers productivity. You, having analyzed your own approach, might decide that it works well within the confines of your organization or needs adjustment. Many people whose style, training, or need is to consider the feelings of others do not necessarily like people. Often, in fact, those who gush about how much they "love" people actually do not.

3. Alliance builder or joiner. We have talked about the importance of alliances but not the how-tos of building them. First, ask yourself if you are generally an alliance builder or if you tend to join a group only after others have already gotten together. For example, if you hear that flextime is going to be initiated but that it won't directly affect your department, do you get a reading on how others feel and trade views with them, or do you sit back and quietly watch events unfold? Some companies encourage joiners, especially among employees who are transferred at regular intervals. It is a way of integrating newcomers into a constantly changing environment. This is often set up as a "buddy" program with a new employee assigned to someone for informal orientation. Answer the following statements with a yes or no.

A. I think that if I keep up with my coffee group, I will have all the news and friends that I need.
B. I cultivate or can identify my counterparts in the company's branches.
C. People generally seek me out to ask questions, share information, or just to socialize.
D. People can predict my opinions on important issues.

E. In the past two years I have added new people to my network.

If you answered yes to B, C, and E and no to A and D, you are a builder. If you answered yes to A and D and no to B, C, and E, you are a joiner.

4. Upward reacher or downward controller. If you are a tender, you may find that you look beneath you on the ladder to see how your subordinates are performing. If your style is strongly political or project-oriented, you may concentrate more on what is going on above you. However, the differences are more subtle. Answer yes or no to the following statements.

A. In my office my boss and I often dress in the same style and often buy clothes from the same retailers.

B. My subordinates follow my lead in dress.

C. My peers seem very much like me in their professional and personal styles.

D. At least one of the top management people in my company graduated from or attended the same college I did.

E. I live in the same geographic area as my colleagues.

F. In the past year there have been no departmental decisions that I strongly disagreed with.

If you answered no to B and C and yes to A, D, E, and F, you are an upward reacher. If you answered no to A, D, E, and F and yes to B and C, you are a downward controller.

SUMMARY

Your responses to the questions and statements in this section, and the analysis of these responses, should help you to categorize your personal style. That style grows out of your experiences with what works on the job filtered through your values. Certain personal styles work well with certain professional styles; others wreak havoc on departments and even entire companies. Study the chart on page 70 in order to see whether your personal and professional styles complement each other.

Even if your professional style is incompatible with your personal style, the dichotomy is not necessarily fatal to your career. Some organizations are so eclectic that you can build power anyway.

How do people see you? At the beginning of this chapter we suggested that your style as you see it may not match what others see. Here are some of the ways to test your assumptions about your style.

1. Find a clone. Whom do you see as most like you stylistically? Ask others how they see that person in terms of style. Never ask them if they like the person. That is irrelevant to what you are testing. Instead, talk openly about style. Does the person have a decisive, command, or social worker style? Ask why that individual thinks so. If the grapevine picks this up, whoever is the object of all this attention is likely to believe you see him/her as a role model. One of the bottom lines of office politics is that any kind of aberrant behavior can be tolerated as long as there is some sort of explanation. Do not be surprised if you and the two to five people you consult do not agree. Disregard

MATCHING PROFESSIONAL/PERSONAL STYLES

Professional Style	Works well with	Does not work with
Consensus	All prestige conscious	Loner, alliance builder
Sales	All	Prestige, loner
Decisive	Problem-oriented, alliance builder, loner, upward reacher, prestige conscious	Alliance joiner
Political	People-oriented, alliance builder, joiner, upward or downward reacher, indifferent	Loner, problem-oriented, prestige
Manipulative	People-oriented	Loner
Social Worker	People-oriented	Loner
Command	Loner	People-oriented, alliance builder, joiner
Fire Fighter	People-oriented	Problem-oriented
Legal/Tight	Loner, problem-oriented	People oriented
Abdication/Weak	Loner, alliance joiner	People-oriented, alliance builder
Secretive	Loner, alliance joiner, downward builder, downward controller	People/problem-oriented, alliance builder
Conditional	Loner, alliance joiner, downward controller	People-oriented, upward reacher

any input if each person you query expresses a different view point; this indicates that the person you picked to study has no dominant style.

2. Who is your guru within the office? Is there a co-worker, preferably older and not a direct competitor, who can give you some feedback on what she/he sees as your

style? Do not ask someone in personnel or employee assistance for such feedback. It has to be from someone who has regular contact with you in work situations. A peer would be most helpful, but a former boss or a very shrewd secretary could help. Ask them what style they think you have. Do not ever tell them what you think because if you do so, they may be tempted to agree with you. This would negate the value their input might have had for you.

If there is no one at work you can trust or who has really seen you work enough (let us say you just started this job) to give feedback, look to your trade or professional society. If you have been a member for several years, you should have been involved in activities such that someone has seen you work. If not, how about someone from your previous job? Your style tends to remain constant over time unless you are forced to change or decide to change. If you are comfortable with a particular approach, only discomfort— and usually quite a lot of it—will cause you to change.

3. Check your past performance appraisals for clues. If you neglected to save these, ask the personnel department for copies. If they want to know why you want them, say, "I'm going to use them to improve my performance!" Reanalyze the written comments in light of this chapter. What did "needs to be more aggressive" mean? You know the situation and the person who made that comment. Did he or she mean you should be more decisive, indicating that was not your style at the time? Did you at the time of the appraisal think the comment irrelevant? Did you choose to disregard it, or did you think of changing jobs because of it? Look for other comments which give you some insight into others' opinions.

It is irrelevant whether you think these comments were "fair" or were prompted by mean-mindedness. They reflect someone's perception—and that is worth noting. If the comments are consistent, it generally means your behavior at that time was consistent. Not every remark can be explained away by mean-mindedness!

4. Listen, not to the words but to the language people use in talking with you. If several or a majority of people in your office treat you in a particular way, they are telling you something very important. How do they approach you? Are they packaging their thoughts for your benefit? Are you one of those people others speak of as emotional, high-strung, or calm? If people consistently treat you in a particular way, it is a clear response to your style.

Suppose your research is a great surprise. Apparently what you believed to be your style is not what others see at all. You think you are a thoughtful, no-nonsense person. They think you are sullen and tactless. What do you do? You have two choices. You can adjust your style, or you can change your work theater to a place where people share your self-perceptions. There are many people, apparently not working in your office, who would recognize a no-nonsense style in that way. Your goal was to build a power base in the office. If this office is not the right environment, then your first job should be to find an environment that is. If you do not, you will never be powerful and your actions will always be misinterpreted.

It is very painful to discover that others do not see you as you see yourself. It is better to experience that pain now rather than find out months or years from now that you have been in an environment where you could never be powerful—your style was at odds with your co-workers and with the organization's. It is either pain up front or failure down the road.

If you and your co-workers agree on your style, you are

ready to move to the actual process of acquiring power. If not, decide what, if anything, you will change. Having done that, you are ready to compare your style with the organization's.

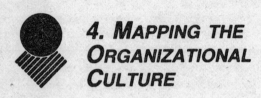

4. MAPPING THE ORGANIZATIONAL CULTURE

TWO advertising agencies serving very similar clients have offices in the same Los Angeles complex. At one, the emphasis is clearly on marketing. A new wave of eager harvard MBAs with marketing majors arrives each spring ready to revolutionize the selling of soap, cigarettes, and beer. They have graphs, matrices, and three-piece suits mass-produced by Brooks Brothers. Six stories below, Harvard MBAs are anathema. The mere mention of business degrees causes the agency's CEO to rant loudly. No one with an MBA from any school has been hired in six years. The company demands either consumer product or small agency experience. All account executives must come up through the creative departments such as art or copy so they will have "a commitment to creativity." The route to power in either agency is different, but the analytical process would be the same. It would start with a careful study of the culture.

Imagine that you are a cultural anthropologist following

in the late Margaret Mead's footsteps. You are about to embark on an important journey, an expedition that will give you insight into a very special culture—your company's. Until now you may not have thought that it was practical or even feasible to study your work environment as an anthropologist would. Few people have. This expedition, if successful, will help you to understand how and why the informal system works. The knowledge you acquire from this environmental study will help you to predict events, build power, and have more control over your work life.

Your aim is to create a map of your organization's culture by investigating its values, traditions, styles, and leadership. By map we mean an understanding of the total culture. Every organization has a unique history; your job is to discover it. The written history, although interesting, is highly unlikely to deal with power relationships. There is nothing written by any company about itself which is balanced; every organization has an idealized view of itself. The official literature does not contain deliberate lies, it is just incomplete or biased.

You, as a power builder, have to uncover a different kind of truth, one that is not available for publication but which can be used for personal and professional purposes. You will need to talk with people and observe them as they work. Do not worry that this task will take up so much time that you will not be able to do your job. You will soon be able to decipher what is worth looking at or listening to and what is not.

Fifty percent of your research time will always be spent on listening to others. You will make your job much more difficult if you start with assumptions. The key to obtaining accurate data is to start with a clear mind. Never give off signals about what you want people to say. Never let them know what you are looking for. Even if you have been with the company for five years and have circulated more than most people, you still have an imperfect overall picture of the company. You must treat this research as if you were an objective outsider, with no stake in the outcome, or you will end up making critical decisions based on subjective data. Objectivity is an acquired skill; you will need it in every aspect of power building. As you begin to study your organization, you should refer to the information in chapter three regarding work styles and work relationships, in order to help you identify the styles of the constituents of the power structure in your company.

Organizations have distinct personalities. They are much more than the sum of the individuals who work within them. Some organizations, such as owner/founder businesses, may reflect only one point of view. Any eccentricity may be embalmed within an organization if someone powerful initiates it. For example, for years a certain newspaper gave female employees a one-pound box of chocolates for Christmas because the editor in chief thought that this was a suitable gift. The tradition continued long after he had died. It did not occur to the management to change this outdated tradition until the paper underwent a major reorganization. It was only at this point that the organization ceased to give Christmas presents to anyone.

Research is like a snapshot. It freezes a moment in time. Organizations are dynamic, however, and even in "stable" companies, everything is continually in flux. Organizations change both deliberately and in response to catalysts. These changes are not always predictable. You only need to study the changes that alter the culture significantly. Look at the ones that provoke resistance or change values and power relationships.

THE CAUSES OF
CULTURAL CHANGE

There are three major forces that cause cultural change: changes in top and middle management; market forces; and deliberate individual influence.

Changes in management: Changes in management are unimportant if the new person's style is similar to the former person's style. However, when a new person exhibits a different style, power will polarize around the new and the old until people have had enough time to evaluate and respond. For instance, the new plant manager likes regular staff meetings, and he expects everyone who attends to contribute ideas. The old plant manager rewarded good soldiers. Under the old regime the winners of the Gary Cooper Taciturnity Contest were stars. In the new regime two gregarious supervisors will stand out. By changing managers the company may be signaling, "This is a new cultural pattern." But change can sometimes result in mixed signals, as top management in its search for "new blood" or "radical change" often forgets that radicals can wear vested suits and new blood may occur in females. Cultural change may be as stereotypical as under the old regime.

If the supervisors find the new manager sufficiently punishing toward the old style, they have three options. They can resist, leave the company, or adapt. They can resist by fighting back through the grapevine. They might cut the new boss out of the informal intelligence network or, if he makes mistakes, see that the grapevine gets the most damning details. Within three months' time you will be able to see if the culture has changed. The supervisors will either be contributing in staff meetings or the meetings will stop. It is difficult to predict which one will happen, but there is no middle ground. That is why so many managers, if they are trying to change the culture, try for some early victories or coups on a new job. If they don't change things right away, they tend to find it becomes harder to initiate change.

Market forces: Profound changes in the culture can occur if manufacturers and salesmen believe a product, even though currently profitable, is either obsolete or no longer competitive. That belief can change the culture. For example, the Wixy company had always made the highest quality commercial snap fasteners. Until recently Wixy had no American competition; the other companies had recognized Wixy's domination of the snap fastener market and had conceded the market. Enter a Japanese firm with a better fastener.

Wixy panics needlessly and begins to reorganize. Without a clue as to what, if anything, can or should be done, the company culture is reworked. Wixy's sales manager is forced to take early retirement, and the marketing department is fired en masse. The president and the board of directors meet weekly. The president is ultimately fired. Concurrently, clones of the previous management are brought in. The resultant culture is so profoundly changed that the new management's first major task is to reinstate the old culture. This situation is as dangerous for a company as random surgery is for a human being.

Individual influence: Gandhi's message that one person has the capacity to cause profound change holds true for organizations as well as nations. The individual who changes the organizational culture may be either someone with a cause or someone willing to fight for what he or she believes is a better way. Sometimes change is initiated without apparent reason. When this happens the resultant cultural change is not the only one that the initiator causes. The entire culture is affected because the change allows all the employees to see themselves in a new light.

Remember when you first heard that a few secretaries were refusing to make coffee? It was not an organized movement. One woman, probably one with considerable tact, may have suggested that the "pleasure" should be spread around. Soon that suggestion became the rule. This small act of assertiveness changed the culture. Secretaries became a real force that had to be acknowledged. Bosses were labeled as oppressive if they objected to making coffee or if they made this task part of the secretary's job description.

Sometimes cultural change is so subtle that it can only be recognized once you have left the company, worked elsewhere, and then returned. It is comparable to returning from a vacation only to notice that your living room walls, which looked fine when you left home, are really a hideous color. At other times cultural change is cataclysmic, as in a reorganization, buyout, or merger.

EMBARKING UPON YOUR EXPEDITION

The grapevine will be your principal exploration tool, but observation and gut-level responses to what you see and hear are always most important. Remember that if a story in the grapevine seems fantastic, it is probably true if you hear the same story from several sources. Your expedition begins as you attempt to answer the following questions.

1. Describe the overall style of the organization. How does it see itself?

Look at the annual report and the public relations press releases and brochures. How does the organization characterize itself? For example, does the annual report feature photographs of the founders, the owners, or top management? Does it highlight products and services? If it is a nonprofit organization, does it feature the people being helped or those providing the services? Is the emphasis primarily on buildings, facilities, and equipment, or on the geographical location of the corporate headquarters or divisions? Is the emphasis divided among them?

How would you characterize the organization's style? Is it a "nurturing" style (that is, everybody comes up through the ranks)? Is it a "problem-solving" or "competitive" style ("We're going to ice the microchip market by 1986")? Is there emphasis on "civic leadership"? Does management feature collective or individual participation in community activities?

Now study the data for what is not there. Companies make deliberate and selective omissions. They expect people to look at the bottom line instead of analyzing documents for values and style. The end results of a company may bear no similarities to the means used to achieve these ends. You want to discover the company's priorities and the methods used to accomplish its goals.

The best source for perspective on the company is someone who has retired after at least twenty years' service. Retirees are often eager to tutor younger people. By sharing their impressions and insights with you, they can retain influence in the organization and buy a slice of organizational immortality. If you do not personally know anyone who has recently retired, ask a longtime secretary for the name of a recent retiree. You need to get as much detail from this person as possible, so allow yourself several hours to talk. Ask the retiree to share his/her impressions in detail about how present top management acquired power and who lost the struggle.

2. Who within your organization is especially good at packaging ideas for top management?

The person need not be a manager. He or she can be anyone with enough top management contact to have learned packaging skills. People who package ideas well are all aware of one thing—they know that to be accepted ideas must be presented in the right way. This is especially true when the ideas involve major change. For instance, suppose that the president of your company is a groupie. You, because you are a loner, often say to her, "Listen, Jeanne, this morning as I was having a cup of coffee I had a great idea for that new sales promotion campaign." Jeanne, from her orientation, thinks, "Why doesn't Jay understand that his ideas aren't that good?"

Contrast that with saying, "Listen, Jeanne, this morning five of us were sitting around drinking coffee in the cafeteria when we had a terrific idea." "Ah," Jeanne thinks, "this should be worth listening to." The idea has not changed, just its packaging.

Another packaging issue concerns who does the presenting versus what is presented. One secretary carrying bad news to top management may be made a scapegoat, while another one, with the exact same message, is seen as a sympathetic soul in the clutches of hideous circumstance. Your job is to find good packagers and analyze what they do that makes them so effective. Don't expect them to be able to explain why they have chosen that particular style; many of them work on instinct. Effective packaging always indicates something about a company's values and culture.

3. Which (if any) of top management's ideas or pet proj-

ects have died or been murdered during the implementation stage by middle management?

One of the risks inherent in being a middle manager is that there are no longer just one or two people who can sink the ship; there are dozens of them. Top management looks toward the long run, forgetting that what is important to a middle manager is his or her career today. Middle management sabotage is common; it is not limited to companies in trouble. Although this kind of sabotage is considerably less obvious and less frequently discussed than the blue collar sort, it can prove to be just as damaging. Middle managers can, do, and will subvert any changes or projects that they feel damage their territories, relationships, or career prospects. It is easy to see managers doing this in budget preparation, work assignments, and transfers.

For instance, top management identified a comer. How did it happen that the comer, specifically a bright young woman supervisor, was offered a transfer to a geographically undesirable location just as the grapevine took "official" note that she far outshone her boss? Her boss, fearing her potential to seize power from him, used his power to transfer her in order to ensure his present position. Knowing her considerable market value, she left the organization. Mission accomplished.

Past projects will often give clues to middle management consensus. No group, especially one so loosely allied as middle management, will develop a tight consensus, although certain issues will engender unity. Look for changes that strengthen workers at middle management's expense (for example, quality circles—Japanese-inspired, consensus-building groups that result in the dilution of middle management command power). Look for projects that keep middle management from using informal "perks." In one company middle management believed that a couple of weekly long-distance calls on the WATS line were part of the reward system. Top management may restrict the use of an 800 line to official business—and then really enforce it! You should be able to spot events like these and the responses to the events.

Open resistance and lobbying for change are a normal part of organizational life. Some companies have even formalized procedures for changing policies and expect their middle managers to give top management regular feedback. Doing this well can be an important source of power. The grapevine is very sensitive to issues managers dare not resist openly. In some companies more issues are resolved through the grapevine than through formal procedures. For instance, top management hears that there are rumblings of discontent about a proposed policy. The policy is quietly revised.

The most interesting resistance that you will uncover will be passive resistance: the art of ignoring something until it becomes invisible or quietly dies. For instance, a new report form was introduced into a community hospital despite objections from department heads already overwhelmed with paperwork. Initially, each manager faithfully filled them out, even though no one could understand who needed or used the information. Within two months several managers fell behind, pleading the press of work. Within six months only one or two managers still complied with the directive. Angry memos followed. For the next several months half the managers filled out the reports. By the end of the first year no one turned them in. Top management regrouped in order to find a better method for extracting the information.

When top management tries to get information that middle management does not want circulated, all kinds of resistance tactics are used. Ask yourself the following questions.

Are there any patterns of resistance? Does top management consistently propose and middle management consistently dispose? If so, there is an imbalance of power somewhere. Either top management does not really care about the proposals or middle management has taken some hostages. For example, if most decisions move from the top down rather than from the middle up, there is a power problem. Knowing which way power flows informally within the organization will help you to plan your power building strategy.

4. Do all levels of management use the grapevine, or do they individually and collectively ignore it?

The grapevine will always be believed before any "official" news from management. A management that does not use the grapevine does not have a comprehensive picture of the organization. This management is more likely to be surprised by response to formal action because it received no clues from the informal system. You can measure management's informal control and influence by observing how much attention they pay to the grapevine. Do managers act openly on what they hear informally?

For example, when a large manufacturing firm filed for Chapter Eleven, top management worried that this temporary problem would drive key people to seek employment elsewhere. The president of the firm called in each key person and explained the situation. Rumors that several people were about to bolt continued to be very strong in the grapevine. Top management called in several opinion leaders and convinced them that the problem was only temporary. Once this new information traveled through the grapevine, the rumors quieted down. If top management had lied to the grapevine and said, "There is no problem," they would have a credibility problem forever after. People's acceptance of the information taken from the grapevine will depend on rank and file verification by trustworthy co-workers.

5. Who is the organization's senior secretary and to whom does she report?

Secretaries are keepers of the cultural flame. Because they are close to power and are power points individually, they have top management and nonmanagement views they can share with those in the trenches. The secretary who has the most seniority in the company often orients other secretaries to the culture, either directly or indirectly. The other secretaries will learn proper secretarial style from her. The senior secretary has probably lived through numerous changes over the years; now her view of the organization is a comprehensive one. She probably trained the corporate officer she reports to in the ways of the informal system, particularly if he or she came in from the outside.

In nonprofit organizations secretaries are often inherited. The secretary to a university dean remains while the deans are rotated. The secretary may be far more powerful informally than her boss and may train him or her in the dean's role. Such a person has more influence on the culture than many people of far higher rank. She may scuttle her boss if he varies too much from the established pattern.

6. Can you identify any people, other than secretaries, who are inordinately powerful for the positions they hold?

Certain jobs are situationally very important. A maintenance supervisor in a hotel has more power than someone with the same job in a manufacturing concern. Hotel guests can leave if room conditions displease them; factory workers grumble but stay.

Do some of the power jobs involve control of a scarce resource other than money, such as mail distribution, word processing, or photocopying? Look at the number of people who want or need a service and then observe how efficiently that service is provided in your organization. In the past ten years word processing has become pivotal in many corporations. Because every world processing system requires its operators to be trained before they can use the equipment, control of the service carries great power. Most people cannot train themselves on the equipment; they are at the mercy of the person with the knowledge.

7. How powerful is the personnel function in the organization? Is the head of personnel a vice-president in fact or in name only? Do managers interview people sent to them informally without fearing reprimands or reprisals from the personnel director?

Personnel has an homogenizing, constricting effect on organizations. If the personnel director has personal power in the informal system, rather than mere position power, the whole department will be strengthened. If top management sees the personnel director as a peer of the word processing supervisor, that is, as simply a service provider, the culture will be different than if the personnel director can impose policies on line managers.

Personnel managers often assume power and importance if the company has trouble remaining nonunion or has civil rights problems. The number of recent sexual harassment suits has strengthened the personnel department. The department as a whole is strengthened if women, who have strong cases for lawsuits, seek help from personnel first and personnel quietly resolves their problems. If managers hire and fire without interference, while personnel picks up the pieces and does the paperwork, the culture is freer but also more volatile.

8. Has the company been through a reorganization in the past three years? What changes in direction can you identify as a result of this reorganization?

Reorganizations are not always prompted by financial problems. They do not have anything to do with takeovers or mergers. Usually it is a desperate attempt to get the company moving. An informal survey of top management people, who were involved in reorganizing divisions within the past few years, revealed the following information. Most of these managers admitted that it was the only way they could think of to break up entrenched power, introduce new ideas, and give middle management a good shaking up. "It improved our productivity immediately," one CEO said. "It made me think that terror and fear for one's job have been underrated as management tools."

Who lost and who gained power in the reorganization? Look for two patterns that indicate style changes. First, is the new management any different demographically (for example, younger, older, better educated, more social) than the old management? Second, can you see signs of a clear rejection of accepted practices? For example, have there been any changes in the benefit package or in executive perks which indicate that the company thinks different incentives are needed?

One of the most common reorganization techniques is to overhaul the management compensation plan. This tells you that top management thinks the plan is insufficiently motivating. Look for clues as to what has changed. Younger managers may find discussion of pensions a gigantic yawn; they want cash, stock, training programs, and glamorous

travel, while managers over fifty may spend hours lovingly
reading the details of the pension plan.

Another common change is to combine departments
which, although redundant, have remnants of powerful internal support. By leaving the newly married to fight it out
for control, management weakens both. It is then compar-
atively simple to get rid of all the emotionally exhausted
survivors on the grounds of low productivity. In the sheer
struggle for survival and control the people will let the work
slide.

9. Have any innovations been resisted by employees,
forcing management to retreat in order to rethink its policies?
Does management now pretend that these innovations were
never introduced?

Rank and file resistance to technical innovation is never
as serious a power problem as resistance to changes in
relationships. For instance, unions may resist robotics on
principle and may negotiate openly for different work rules.
If changes are subsequently made in management style,
reporting relations, and nonphysical conditions, the unions
may go underground and simply resist what has been done
because there probably isn't anything specific to discuss.
For example, there is no protest when a supervisor who is
well liked is replaced with a clone. Watch the fireworks,
however, if the new supervisor wants to "shape things up"
or "get the department under control."

10. What kind of local publicity does the company receive?

Public relations departments usually have warmer ties
with the local than the national press. If the local press has
been talking about the company in ways that you know the
PR department wouldn't authorize, try to find out why. It
is highly unlikely that public relations has lost its touch.

Some new facts have reached the media from a very reliable source, probably someone within the company who is incensed at reading still another fantasy.

SUMMARY

Once you have analyzed the culture in minute (and sometimes boring) detail, you are ready to look at the total picture. In order to do this you need to sum up what you have learned. Does the organization overall seem energetic? Can you feel movement within the culture? It is always easier to build power within an energetic culture. A lethargic culture tends to be stiffer and less responsive.

An energetic culture will often reward people who do anything short of twitching. If managers are geared to action and are rewarded for decisiveness, yet are still expected to be flexible, they will recruit and reward people just like themselves. In a lethargic culture managers reward people who do not "press too hard." If you are a pusher by nature, you cannot be a successful power builder in a lethargic culture. You will be continually frustrated if you attempt to build power in this type of culture. Since every industry has companies all along the style spectrum, your particular style should please several of them.

A great many theories have been created to explain why some people will do well in a particular environment while others in the same environment do poorly. The emphasis previously was on what the company could do to hold on to a variety of personality types and styles. The idea was that variety equaled energy and leavened the organization. Some managers even think that the conflict produced by variety is desirable. The problem with this supposition is that a company is made up of individuals, usually of similar styles. Only top management wants variety; everyone else wants compatibility and smooth working relationships. This explains why the organizational culture must be continually monitored. Sometimes top management succeeds in introducing diversity; at other times middle management keeps the lid on.

After looking at your own and then the company's style, what can you conclude? Is there a match? Are there people on different rungs of the organizational ladder with styles similar to yours? Remember, finding yourself at odds with the organization does not mean that you are likely to be forced out immediately, or even eventually. We are talking about building power, not job security. These are entirely different issues. You can be a nebbish and keep your job until retirement even if no one else in the company has a style even remotely similar to yours. Matching styles and values is only important if you want to build power.

Suppose that you differ stylistically from those in power. You are introspective and fear that they have all graduated from advanced courses in positive thinking. They socialize on the golf course; you jog. They have sports cars; you drive a Land Rover. Is there any hope for you to build power? There may be, if you are willing to tone down your differences. At this point you may think that jogging versus golf should not be an issue at all. The real issue here is not golf versus jogging or sports cars versus Land Rovers. It is a much more practical difference. In order to build power you must appear to be trustworthy. It is harder to trust people who are stylistically different because their behavior is less predictable. For instance, if the co-workers whose cooperation you need the most regularly spend time together playing golf, you will be excluded from the rapport building, the gossip, and the camaraderie which builds mutual trust if you do not play golf.

A university professor coveted the chairmanship of his department. He had a beard, a professional wife, no children, and a quiet, introspective style. His colleagues liked him personally; however, they believed that he was too easygoing to protect their interests with a college dean who seemed to have stepped out of the movie *Patton*. When one of them approached him to inform him that the other professors were inclined to choose a more abrasive, less well liked, colleague for chairman, the professor was hurt. He could not understand what was to him an unfair choice.

If you have accurately analyzed the culture, you should not need to ask anyone what your prospects are. If you believe that you are at variance with the culture, you have the following choices.

1. You can modify your professional style, and even your personal style, if you treat what you do as a role to be acted. You do not have to believe that being outgoing is better or that protocol is the embodiment of the work ethic. You need only act that way in business and quasi-business situations. If you can separate the need to be sincere from the need to appear sincere, you may still be able to build power. However, if you insist on total honesty, and the company doesn't value honesty, you will be very honest but powerless.

2. You can locate and cultivate people within the firm who are stylistically similar to you. If they are a large enough minority, or if those who are like you represent potentially powerful people, you will probably be able to build a power base even if the overall company has a very different style.

3. You can modify your professional but not your personal style. You can socialize only at work and skip the golf games. It will not be as effective as extracurricular

socializing, but it will be better than no modifications at all. You can take charge of the group's social life and plan activities closer to your own style. Remember that if you initiate changes, they will have to adapt!

4. You can ignore the whole thing because the price of change is too high both personally and professionally. That is the bottom line choice. Maybe power is not worth it to you. You cannot or will not adapt. You cannot or will not move. There is still hope. The best research available on the subject indicates that organizations often modify their styles. You can conscientiously do your job and wait for such changes to occur. This is a high risk choice, however, because a job you want may be filled by someone else while you are waiting.

If you decide to modify your personal style, do it in very small increments. If you are radically different on Monday, people will think you were struck by lightning over the weekend. They will watch you intensely lest you be struck again. They will also question you very carefully. That kind of tactic does not build trust. The easiest professional changes to make are to your personal image, that is, your dress and manners, and the way you treat other people. That is just a matter of language. You can change your perceived style from brusque to friendly by altering your language from "Do this" to "Could you please do this." As with all change, once it is initiated it must be consistently done.

Our focus group research dispels the myth that young people are more adaptable than their elders. You have heard that the older one gets, the more one gets set in one's ways. Not so. According to our research, people over forty seemed less passionately committed to a particular professional style than people under forty were. As one man of twenty-five said, "Listen, I'm going to go with this style no matter what." Some people who did change their images also found that blending in with the organizational style was personally more comfortable. Others changed back to their true style as soon as they left the specific organization. Do not expect that knowing the organization's culture will eliminate all mistakes. Instead, use what you know to prevent as many of them as possible and to further your career goals. Having done the research you are now ready to build relationships. The most important power relationship will be with your boss.

5. POWER BUILDING STRATEGIES: INFLUENCING THE BOSS

IF your job depended on it, could you describe your boss in detail—his/her likes, ambitions, fears, interests? Have you treated the boss as someone who, while more powerful than you are, is not really subject to the same analysis you have applied to the rest of the organization? Even if you have "analyzed" the boss, what have you done with that information?

Your analysis of your boss should include a feeling for his/her ambition, style, and most important, a sense of what is missing from his/her work life. For instance, if your boss has been in his/her present job a long time, what does the grapevine indicate is the reason? Is it lack of ambition, or is the boss at odds with the system? Are others static instead of moving ahead within the organization because of a slower growth rate, or is your boss's career stalled while those around him/her move up?

In this chapter we are going to use the data you have

collected to build power with the boss. We are going to learn to influence decisions and, when we reach the limits of influence, to negotiate directly for what we want. Influence means persuading the boss to help you without your agreeing to do anything in return. Negotiation means offering the boss something in return for what you want. (We will explain how to do this with finesse.)

Negotiation will always be the more effective tool, but using influence is the way to begin. After all, if you succeed in influencing the boss to help you in a particular way, you won't need to negotiate! The goal is to get the result as simply as possible. After you have built power with your boss, we will show you how to build power with your peers and subordinates.

STRATEGIES FOR INFLUENCING THE BOSS

Once you have done your analysis, here are some ways to build power with your boss. Each will also make you more productive, a bottom-line need in the 80s. According to the information people give when asked to keep time sheets by quarter hours, few people are actually working productively as much as four out of any eight-hour period. This may explain why productivity is to the 1980s what management by objectives was to the 1970s. It is number one on almost every organization's agenda. Being more productive will be important in your plans and will influence your methods. For instance, each method we suggest will help you plan for a result. Most beneficial, you will be verifying and increasing your practical knowledge of how the system really works, raising your visibility (a power in itself), and if you do it right, not once threatening your boss or his/her feelings of rank or general superiority.

If you threaten your boss in any way, you are not power building; you are raising your risk level and giving your boss a good reason to get rid of you. Everything you do must boost your boss's career while giving you more power or teaching you something you can use to move up or on.

As part of building power, you need to ask yourself the following questions.

1. What unmet needs does your boss have which you can fill? Any discussion of building influence begins here. What isn't your boss getting? What is he/she unable to do for him/herself? Filling in a gap is a primary influence-building tool. For example, if your boss is disorganized and forgetful and you are the opposite, why not bail him or her out? You can do it even if it is not part of your job. Since the boss needs this help anyway, do it without announcing what you are doing. It is always easier to get forgiveness than permission. Your good intentions are clear; that helps reduce fallout from any errors you might make in your zeal. It will also demonstrate your commitment to the department and to your own job.

Object: to have your boss become dependent on you for a special service. Instead of feeling threatened, most bosses will see your effort as personal and professional devotion. This is what the boss wants to believe anyway, and loyalty is never unfashionable. Do not disillusion him or her. You will learn the art of managing up, a very useful skill to employ until you are chairman of the board or CEO some-where. When you arrive there you can teach your subordinates how to do the same thing with you!

2. Can you compensate for a weakness in your boss's style? For instance, suppose your boss is blunt, tactless,

and generally difficult to get along with. Your boss hates people contact and the problems people create. If you assume some of that contact, deal with and satisfy the people your boss most dislikes, these people will soon approach you instead of your boss. Unless your boss is more than ordinarily paranoid, he or she is likely to be quite content to let you handle such people. You will then have assumed some of the decision-making power your boss previously had. You become the boss in dealing with those people.

Many people, especially many women, feel that working for a difficult boss, or one who is not well liked by peers and subordinates, is a career negative. They see it as a threat to career mobility. The opposite seems to be true when productivity is used to determine who moves up. According to the April 1983 edition of *Room at the Top*, a newsletter published by Ned Klumph Associates in Cherry Hill, New Jersey, "Domineering, often hostile managers usually get productive results." It may not be warm and comfortable, but it is an opportunity to build power by working with someone whose results are much better than his/her peers.

Object: to motivate others to trade with you by filling a personal or professional gap. This gives you some control over a chunk of your boss's job. Filling in a gap can help you learn to manage when no other learning opportunity exists and changing jobs is not an immediate possibility. If your boss decides he or she wants those contacts back, give them back. It will not reduce the influence you have acquired. The people you have helped will still be your allies because power cannot be transferred from someone who fulfills the needs of others to someone who cannot or will not. As long as you do not violate protocol by building an obviously competitive power center, you will have no problem. Do not worry about getting "credit."

3. Can you help your boss's career? Yes, but not by calling dear old Uncle Ned and asking him to talk to his contacts among the company's board of directors. It is more effective to do some judicious internal public relations for your boss. This may seem elementary, but very few people do it. Those who do so stand out. You not only create an aura around your boss, but your image will reflect the light.

For instance, your boss may not be plugged into several important grapevines. It is axiomatic that as you move up the ladder there are fewer opportunities to regularly "debrief" the rank and file. Some executives simply find it more trouble than it is worth. Others are so concerned with peer and top management networks that they lack the time to keep up with the trenches. By seeing that your boss's achievements get into the grapevine you boost him or her, the department, and most especially yourself. You also become an early warning system for the boss because most bad news starts in the trenches. The secretaries, janitors, and maintenance people get the news first.

As others recognize you as a news source they will come to rely on what you tell them. As people make decisions based on your information you will become more powerful. Since your boss is bound to hear of the work you have done in his or her behalf, there is not much danger of misinterpretation. It would take an exceptional boss to figure out that you were doing yourself equally as much good. Even if he or she did figure out your method and motives, what coul he do? Most company policies do not include firing an employee for speaking well of his or her superior under the category "firing for cause." All this assumes your boss is doing a good, or at least adequate, job. If not, preserve a judicious silence. Any publicity when someone has a performance problem is bad publicity.

Object: to gain control over sources of information about neglected areas of the company and also your department and to become the primary conduit for the information going outside the department. The opening wedge is generalized positive publicity about your boss, whose actions are usually of the greatest interest to people outside the department.

When Mary Noble joined the hospital supply company, her boss warned her that the company was very "gossipy. Rumors are the only interest of more than half the staff," he said sourly. "Just stay out of it." In fact, Mary kept her head down the first six months but she listened intently. Three months later her boss began to question her about what she was hearing. The company was planning to consolidate several departments, possibly the one Mary worked in, and the boss needed information. Without letting on that she had deliberately ignored his instructions, she was able to fill him in. Three months later, at her anniversary review, she got the largest raise in the department. The boss now looks to her for occasional readings—he still dislikes routine "gossip"—and rewards her appropriately.

4. Teaching the boss his/her job is a source of great power, but it is also a source of as great or greater risk. George Bernard Shaw once said, "Those who can, do, those who can't, teach." He was wrong. Those who cannot do a thing well cannot teach anyone else to do it well either. Herein lies the power and also the trap in being assigned to train a boss. Generally there are destructive politics at work in such situations. The person who is doing the training ought to have been named manager, but something, usually a political problem, prevented it.

Suppose your new boss is brought in from another department or from outside the company. You are assigned by his boss to "orient" him. For a short period of time you have the new boss's career in your hands. Since you give the boss information, you can shape that information in a manner that creates a dependency in the boss. If you neglect to show him how your department's informal system works, or how other informal systems which he needs work, you set him up to fail. If you do this, you will risk retaliation if, against the odds, he succeeds anyway. This happens more often than anyone likes to acknowledge, especially those making such delicate assignments.

Do not be tempted to orient the boss selectively; it is a self-defeating strategy. If the boss is going to fail, he should do it on his own. If you facilitate the process, you still cannot be sure you will be named manager. Having been passed over once does not augur well for your promotability in the organization.

Once the new boss feels relatively confident that he commands the facts about the job, he will almost certainly fire the subordinate who provided the training; to keep the subordinate poses a threat to the new boss's command power. Only if the new boss is certain that his subordinate has provided him with solid information about the internal system does that subordinate stand a chance. This is never discussed openly but is often spoken of as "loyalty" or being a "team player." After all, the new boss is as much a victim in this game as the subordinate. If the subordinate really wants the manager's job, the best strategy would be to apply for it elsewhere.

The subordinate gains in several ways by effectively teaching the new boss the job, as completely as possible. While the training is going on the subordinate is likely to have a conduit to the boss's boss who will expect progress reports. This expands the subordinate's network into otherwise inaccessible areas. Biilding that relationship can be a powerful deterrent to later reprisals by the new boss. "After all," the new boss reasons, "my boss thought enough of this person to have him/her train me. There may be a tighter relationship there than I supposed."

In addition, all of the power inherent in the job will not go with the boss once both boss and subordinate have assumed their assigned positions on the organization chart. The subordinate will retain some influence over the boss, if only as an informal adviser and keeper of the department's history. Others in the department may consult the subordinate surreptitiously because they realize he or she still knows as much as, possibly more than, the new boss. It may take the new boss a year or more to consolidate his control. In governmental agencies many managers, often executive appointees, never learn enough about the system to establish control.

Object: to shape the boss in ways useful to one's own career while training him or her. This entails considerable risk because, if the boss feels threatened enough, the trainer is going to be out as soon as the boss secures his or her position. Shaping the boss is also an opportunity to consolidate and rationalize one's own grasp of how the system works. The hidden bonus here is that the subordinate has actually done the manager's job and should be able to get the same or a similar job elsewhere.

5. Getting things done efficiently and anticipating your boss's desires is always a form of power. Before you protest that any competent person would do that, ask yourself how often you do so. How many times do you wait to be asked or even ordered to do something? Passivity is powerlessness, and waiting is acknowledgment of the condition. You are not directing and therefore not in control. If you learn to think like your boss, anticipate what he/she will want, and

do it before you are asked, you will create a dependency. People whose professional lives are very comfortable are loathe to disturb the arrangements. They are likely to reward such overachievers but will not promote them. That would be counterproductive. Why make oneself uncomfortable? You have to look after your own advancement. More important, by taking on more work you create new learning opportunities for yourself. Where is that kind of learning available except on the job? Ten courses in planning, problem solving, and organizational behavior will leave your eyes glazed over and your career at the gate. A more pragmatic educational program helps move you forward.

Object: to anticipate the boss's wants so you can pick off the plum career building and learning experiences while handing the boss a beautiful and useful fait accompli. This is a crowd pleaser and likely to obscure the power building aspects from the boss's view. Some of your peers will notice, so prepare to be copied.

6. Scheherazade was no fool. The person who can shape a story into something memorable and gripping, and who can point out the political implications and pitfalls of information in a nonthreatening way, will never be powerless. Executive secretaries are frequently masters at this. We have said before, but it is always worth repeating, the higher up you are on the ladder, the harder it is to stay plugged in to the internal network. A person who wanted to build power with a boss could become a purveyor of the finest facts and most interesting rumors circulating both inside and outside the company. He or she can make the boss dependent because the boss needs and usually wants that information without having to dig for it.

This strategy will work only if the boss and subordinate trust each other. It should never be attempted if the boss feels threatened by a subordinate or cannot stand to hear bad news. You will know how your boss feels instantly by his/her reaction to any bad news you relay. An ostrich complex is a terrible flaw in a boss, although a common one. Stand aside and the boss may sink quietly, done in by a crisis he/she ignored. Unless both boss and subordinate can depend on the accuracy of the information as well as anticipate each other's reaction, relaying information cannot be used for power building.

Do not use this strategy with a boss who has an insatiable appetite for pure (personal) gossip. If your boss really cares about who got drunk at the last golf outing, you will spend more time information gathering than working. You will create enemies, plus the temptation to "create" juicy rumors is enormous. This will ultimately allow you to be fired for cause, that is, for not doing your assigned job.

Another kind of important information has become an issue between bosses and subordinates. Many top management people suddenly find themselves dependent on others for information because they do not know enough about computers to access the organization's information system independent of the people in data processing. Since access is always a source of power, a clever subordinate would learn enough about the organization's information system to assist the boss in getting information directly, simultaneously helping him/herself keep abreast of changing technology. There is no successful company so small that it will not have a computer by 1985. BASIC is the language of microcomputers. Have you taken a course yet? If not, how will you maintain your own power base in the next few years? If you are cut off from computer information, market and strategic forecasts, and accounting information, you have a problem even though much of this information eventually turns up in the grapevine. What will you do if you need more complete or more immediate facts?

Object: to establish a relationship with the boss based on supplying suitably packaged, necessary internal information. Never censor rumors because you think that the boss might not like to hear them. When the boss hears directly of an impending holocaust, rumors of which you suppressed, you will be politically dead. You may even be fired. It requires both integrity and courage to carry information, but this is an almost foolproof route to power. Since technology is often difficult for people with position power to adapt to, keep your boss current about developments. New ways to use technology, which you discover, can help ease the transition. You will still know more about the technology than the boss, and that is a major source of power which will make you more valuable.

BUILDING POWER THROUGH NEGOTIATING

You have done everything we suggested to influence the boss's thinking. You have had some success, but so far you seem to be working very hard and are without as great a payoff as you would like. Now that you have built a good working relationship with your boss, what steps are necessary in order to make it more useful to your career? Whether you define useful as moving up or holding on, now is the time to learn to negotiate.

Someone once said that all human relationships are negotiated. That is, everything we either give or get must be bartered for—cooperation, friendship, love, upward mobility, and job longevity. It is true. You can influence people positively, but you are still in the realm of indirect action. We need something more direct, more controllable.

Negotiating is the process of exchanging something for something else. Usually what you are exchanging is very different from what you hope to get. After all, there would not be much point in exchanging one ten dollar bill for another just like it or even for two fives. As a process, negotiating is neither good nor bad; it is neutral. It is a process for coming to terms with or for reaching an agreement which is satisfactory to all involved. The negotiating you do will be nonmonetary and usually involves trading a special service for a decision.

Negotiating should be a win/win proposition. You and the person with whom you are negotiating must have an equal stake in the outcome. That is the incentive to meet each other's needs. In fact, that is the most important point about negotiating for power. Both sides must feel that they received at least seventy-five percent of what they wanted; otherwise there is no compelling reason to fulfill the bargain. It is too easy to have a "change of heart." Compromises rarely work because they do not provide enough of a payoff to satisfy everyone involved, and they make those involved feel compelled to give specific performances.

Negotiating does not depend on brilliance or quickness of wit. The keys are practice and preparation—which is why many plodders use the process so well. Information is always an important chip in negotiations. As you negotiate you will be trading news for power or even trading different kinds of information. Anything that someone else wants and you can supply is a legitimate bargaining chip. It is not up to you to decide what someone should want, simply to meet the need that is there. You will discover unmet needs through observation, the grapevine, and sometimes just listening to the person lament.

USING NEGOTIATION TO GET WHAT YOU WANT

Suppose your boss is about to make assignments for projects which will keep four supervisors, including you, busy for the next six months. You are particularly interested in two of the four assignments. You have debriefed your sources and are reasonably sure your boss has not made a final decision. How can you influence your boss to give you your first choice when you are not her favorite and your three peers are likely to want the same assignment? Furthermore, the four of you have interchangeable skills; all of you could do the job equally well. Whatever method your boss uses to make decisions, it will be a personal, not a professional, choice. Your job is to convince your boss that giving you your first choice would be in her and the department's best interests.

Here are five ways you could approach this problem. Let us examine each so you will see how each works, its weaknesses, and generally why negotiating is the best tool.

1. Ask the boss for the assignment outright. You can do this by saying, "I'd like a crack at that project," or you can present an elaborate game plan of how you would handle the project if it were assigned to you. This might work. However, if you truly are not the boss's favorite, she may decide you have breached protocol. No one has asked you for a preference. She might assign you the least desirable

project (from your viewpoint) to remind you not to make the same mistake again. Her negative reaction to your request might spill over into other areas of your working relationship.

2. You can let the grapevine know you are hot for a particular assignment, counting on this information to get back to your boss and influence her decision. She might take this into account, or she might ignore it. The grapevine, while accurate, is still part of the informal system. It can never be proven that she heard the rumor or heard it in the form you intended.

3. Instead of trying to influence your boss, you can work through your peers, letting them know how much you want the assignment. If you have built strong relationships with them they may back off or even root for you. However, even if your boss knew about these machinations, she might not be influenced by them. She might resent your campaign, and that could endanger your working relationship. Her department is not a democracy!

4. You can try to influence your peers to turn down the assignment you want. In exchange, you will help them on their projects or provide some other reward. This puts them at risk with the boss but, if one or more are willing to do this, you might get the project by default. If a peer takes such a large risk of angering the boss, she/he will expect something major in return, probably several major things. It may be a case of your agreeing to do the same for him or her in the future.

5. You could try to reach your boss's boss through his secretary. If you have a long-standing relationship with her, she might try to help. This is a risky strategy, however, because if your boss finds out, she might rightly interpret

your effort as an attempt to move around her. Also, you can usually count on a boss's boss supporting the boss and declining to interfere in such a matter.

Unfortunately, none of these methods has a high probability of success. In any kind of power building, the more indirect the method is, the greater the number of people who will be involved, the more complicated the transaction will be, and the more prone to failure your effort will be through misunderstanding of the method. The obvious solution is to approach the boss directly with negotiation in mind.

THE NEGOTIATION MINDSET

Every good negotiator, not to mention good politician, approaches whatever he or she wants to negotiate in one way. He or she asks the question, "What can I do for the other person that will make him or her want to do it my way?" You start not with what you want but with what the other person is likely to want. If you can train yourself to think this way, you will literally leap over your competitors who are probably stuck in a mindset which always begins with, "How can I get what I want?"

If you are to do this, you will need to reorganize and reanalyze the information you have collected. Ask yourself, "What could my boss want?" You then negotiate to fill in the blanks. If you don't feel surfeited with recognition and appreciation, it is safe to assume that no one else does either. Are you getting total career building help? Is your understanding of the informal system complete?

Back to our original problem. What would make her want

to give you the assignment? How do you show her that giving you the assignment is in her own best interests? You can find out only by discussion, making offers and getting rejections, in other words, negotiating.

How is negotiating different from influencing the boss? It is much more direct. Instead of quietly and without any quid pro quo doing things far beyond the job description, we are going to talk with her in terms of exchange. Be forewarned: the word negotiation is taboo. Universally it conjures up thoughts of labor unions. We are using the term because it is necessary in order to accurately explain the process. There is no need to get people excited by a word that has so much excess baggage. All you will get is a knee-jerk reaction that colors what you are trying to do. Once you have finished reading this chapter, you will exclusively use the word "discuss." You will say to your boss, peer, or subordinate, "Let's discuss this."

RESEARCHING A NEGOTIATION PROBLEM

Let us assume your boss has not been thinking deeply about how she will assign the new projects. That task is on a mental back burner waiting for more input, an inspiration, or just time to think strategically. This means that the situation is still fluid enough for you to influence her decision. The time to move is now. Here are the preparatory steps.

1. Recheck the grapevine. Bring your boss's name up casually at lunch with a nice but neutral remark. Someone, possibly her secretary or a colleague's secretary, knows what your boss is not currently satisfied with and may mention it to you. You need to know these things and make a list.

(Others may have ideas as well.) This will take a few days because you will have to be circulating in the coffee room and at lunch in order to accumulate this information. Eventually you may learn that your boss does not feel her boss appreciates her work. She feels cut off from what others in the organization are doing and saying because she often skips lunch to catch up on her projects. She does not feel her career is moving quickly enough, and she doesn't know how to publicize her successes without sounding as if she is bragging. Put any ideas that occur to you on the list too. You have been working with her for some time. Think back to casual remarks she has made which reveal an attitude. Now that you have some ideas, what do you do?

2. Construct a negotiating grid. This is a written list of options done in grid form which will help you prepare for your meeting with her. (See the diagram below.) You are going to fill in the blanks.

I WANT	I (CAN) GIVE
(S)HE WANTS	(S)HE (CAN) GIVE

You know what you want. You want your first choice assignment. Failing that, you will take second, third, or fourth. Always list what you want in order of declining importance and work down. When you are negotiating up the ladder, it is confusing if someone is not direct and will prolong the discussion. We are interested in matching needs, not in playing games. In other negotiating situations you might have different priorities, especially if money were involved. What is appropriate here is straightforward, precise thinking.

You can list what your boss wants or what she seems to want. That is also fairly simple. Now, what do you put in the space that says I Can Give? Well, what could you do to help your boss's career? Can you give her a boost? If you can, how do you let her know you will do it?

You can help her by publicizing her professional achievements in the grapevine. You may have done some of this already but not in a systematic way. Because she has not done more self-publicity does not mean she is not interested in it. It does make a difference how quickly news gets to decision makers, such as her boss. If you are actually working at gathering and dispensing information, you can sell that.

So far we have four things. From the information you gathered from the grapevine you know your boss (1) does not feel her boss appreciates her work, (2) feels cut off from what others in the organization are doing and saying, (3) does not feel her career is moving quickly enough, and (4) does not know how to publicize her successes without bragging. Now you know how you can help your boss's career: You can give her a boost. You can let her know you will do it, and then you can help her by publicizing her professional career. You know your boss at least well enough so that you should be able to add other items to the list. You will need about ten or twelve items; otherwise, if none is immediately appealing to her, you and she will not strike a deal.

What she can give is clear: She can assign you the project of your choice or, if not that, your second choice. She can rearrange some elements, in concert with you, to give you a slightly different project. Given enough incentive, she might even restructure all of the projects along the lines you suggest. Do not for a minute think this cannot and does not happen. Bosses frequently accept and work from a subordinate's agenda, if the subordinate provides compelling reasons to do so. Now look at what you have.

I WANT	I CAN
First choice assignment	Help her career
Second choice assignment	Give her a boost
Third choice assignment	Let her know I will do that
	Publicize her career

SHE WANTS	SHE CAN
Appreciation for her work	Give first choice assignment
Interaction with co-workers	Give second choice assignment
Her career to move more quickly	Rearrange elements for slightly
Her career to be more publicized	different project
	Restructure all of the projects
	along lines I suggest

The grid is your first negotiating tool. You now have the outline of the discussion you are going to have with your boss. Contrast this with going in to the boss and asking for the project outright, telling her your needs, while meeting none of hers. Don't you think you are in a stronger position now? Remember, she is a human being with human attributes. She may change her mind about you entirely and decide you are not so bad as she had previously thought. Her change in attitude will be a result of what you have done!

SETTING UP THE MEETING

It is time to talk to your boss. You see her in the hall and say, "Can we get together for a few minutes today or tomorrow? I wanted to bring you up to date on what's going on." You need not mention the projects at this time since that would give her an opening to cut you off. Suggest that the two of you have coffee. It will increase your effectiveness (and confidence) if you meet anywhere but across the desk in her office.

At this meeting you will bring her up to date, as you pledged, on what you are doing. Then you say, "I've been thinking that our department doesn't get the kind of recognition it should. The grapevine doesn't seem to carry our successes nearly as often nor as strongly as it should." This is your opening statement. You are giving her a chance to agree, disagree, or dismiss this as a problem. She says, "I know, but I wasn't sure it was a major problem." Now you can begin the real negotiations.

Say, "I know you haven't made assignments for the second half projects yet, but I've been thinking about it. Aren't there some ways to exploit those projects as publicity opportunities for the department? For instance, if you assign me to the ABC project, I would work at letting people know how well things are going." This is your opening offer. Without challenging her in any way, you have said, "If you assign me this project, I'll do publicity for the department and, by implication, for you."

If she accepts, she will say something like, "That's a good idea. I think you could do that, and I know you like that sort of thing." She may ask you not to say anything until she announces the assignments. You will agree and respect that confidence. Do not even consider telling your best friend. If the grapevine picks up even a whisper of that news, your credibility will be gone, and you won't be back at the gate but in a hole.

If she does not want more publicity internally, she may say, "I'm not sure publicity is exactly what we need." She is not rejecting you personally, nor is she saying she is not going to give you the project you want. She is asking you for another idea. You make her another offer. You say, "Have you ever thought that part of our invisibility around here may be that Jack [her boss] doesn't really know about what we accomplish? Sometimes he seems to feel we're just a service area, not critical to the organization. Last week, someone at the lunch table said Jack is always sure we're not as productive as we could be, even though he apparently doesn't think we're unproductive overall. I wonder if there aren't some ways that we could let him know, say through the grapevine, that these new projects are highly successful." Again you have made an offer and reminded her about the projects. You and your boss should not have any awkwardness in discussing the grapevine. Just provide an explanation of method and of your idea if you and she have never talked openly about office networks.

"I like that idea," she says. "I'd like some ideas on how we should do that. How about Friday?" You say, "Sure, I'll think about it right away. When will you be making assignments?"

At this point your boss may or may not say that you will get your first choice. She may wait to see what you will do between today and Friday. However, you have given her an incentive to give you your first choice. The kind of effort she wants from you is not part of the job. She cannot command you to enthusiastically work your network for the department's benefit. She will expect to provide an incentive, not a payoff. The assignment is her idea of an incentive. If you had said, "May I have the ABC assignment?" you would have breached protocol and made your boss think you expected the assignment as a reward. That smacks of more equality than she, or any boss, can tolerate. You would lose. Instead, by asking for information, you provide a gentle hint with no inchoate threat. The entire process could take fewer than five minutes.

All negotiations with your boss should follow this format. You will always begin with a summation of the past, followed by the first unmet need. You should assume that your boss's interests match the department's interests because that is what he or she assumes! Never, ever imply that you expect a quid pro quo for what you are doing. Your boss would have to have an IQ of 12 not to realize that you are giving something in exchange for something else.

Do not expect that each time you make an offer you will get everything you want. In what relationship does that make sense? You are going to be better off and seen as more powerful than your peers even if only half the things you try work. Remember, although your peers may be trying to build power with your boss, most still believe that problems and opportunities are best attacked with hard work.

The way to keep the negotiations productive and positive is to key all requests to things you really value and all offers to things you can personally deliver. Never offer to trade the efforts or influence of others. You cannot be sure the person will help just because it is critical to you.

WHEN NEGOTIATIONS MAY FAIL

Our goal in negotiating with the boss has been to get something for something. It has been an open process. Occasionally you run into a nonnegotiable situation which will leave you wondering why your boss stonewalled a request which seemed relatively simple to you. Sometimes your boss may even try to force you to do whatever you said you could do without anteing up on his/her side. Here is how to handle some fairly common nonnegotiable situations.

1. When the boss stonewalls you, refuses even to discuss a request, he/she is making a statement. For reasons that may remain obscure to you, you have put the boss on the spot. He or she cannot do whatever it is you have asked for. Pride and the need to preserve authority prevent him/her from mentioning this. You, because you did not see this as a possibility, kept pressing. The boss reacted by closing off discussion and has since refused to reopen discussion of the problem.

Look carefully at the power relationship between the boss and his/her boss. It is possible that your boss has much less decision-making power than you thought. If you keep pressing, you will eventually confirm this, but the price will be quite high. Do not press your boss any further. Go back to your sources and see who does have influence with your boss's boss. Is what you want worth going around your boss to get? It may be that there is no safe or even low-risk way to do that. If so, you are stuck with a nonnegotiable situation.

2. The boss's goal is absolute command, and therefore he/she wants no discussions of any kind. If you keep trying to change the system that he or she has established, your job will be at risk. If two attempts to negotiate fail, you have a boss with a command fixation. You will not be able to find an unmet need greater than your boss's need for absolute domination. However, most people are not that single-minded. The command personality is often such that he/she craves information. You may find that huge quantities of regularly supplied information will help you get what you want.

3. Your boss feels threatened by your effort. He/she is

not against it, just anxious that someone wants something enough to work so very hard for it. Your boss may delight in showing you that hard work does not equal success in any endeavor! Of all the problem bosses, those with sensitive egos are the hardest to deal with.

4. Your boss is subject to enormous peer pressure. He/she feels that if anyone looked over the landscape and your head popped up higher than your peers' heads, it would reflect on his/her control. People with a tremendous need to impress peers often act against their own interests. Nothing much can be done to help them. If your boss is sensitive to public opinion, be sure not to threaten his/her sense of mastery until you have secured another job.

BUILDING ON YOUR SUCCESSES

Once you have mastered the negotiating process, you can use it as often as issues that you want to influence arise. If you then build and maintain with your boss the kind of relationship you need in order to negotiate, you will find it much easier than if you wait until an issue comes up and you are forced to act quickly. Do not expect that your boss will always act in his/her best interests. Maintaining a flexible outlook that acknowledges the possibility of someone's occasional suicide dive allows you to think more creatively. The minute you say to yourself, "I know how he/she will react," you are on the downward slide. People do not always know themselves how they will react, so how can you know?

Practice negotiating until it is automatic. Use the process personally as well as professionally. Your family and friends will respond enthusiastically to this approach. If it is second nature to you, chances are it will be even more effective when you need it.

Once you have established a negotiating relationship with your boss, it is time to work on your peers.

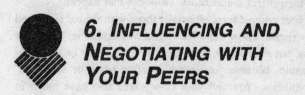

6. INFLUENCING AND NEGOTIATING WITH YOUR PEERS

WHILE Rob Elsworth had known his employer, a paint and chemicals manufacturer, was in trouble, he was appalled to see how much the mere announcement of a corporate reorganization affected the work environment. The management consulting team which was going to restructure the operating areas of the company had not even been chosen when he began to see some of his co-workers engaged in long, clandestine meetings in bars rarely frequented by employees. He saw people closing their doors, and three of his direct competitors began to play golf and pointedly did not ask him to join them even though his was the lowest handicap. He began to feel threatened by people he had previously seen as friends. The reorganization, although it lasted an agonizing three months, really changed very little. Still, Rob continues to look at his co-workers warily.

Any survivor of a company reorganization or merger

would agree that peers (those with the same rank and/or job title) on a vendetta can more effectively damage your career than a displeased boss. They can also cause you twice the personal and professional pain. Fact: About twenty-five percent of the people who are political victims are done in by their direct competitors. How can that happen?

Your competitors, especially those with similar skills and experience, know more about your vulnerabilities than your boss can ever know, regardless of the quality of that relationship, because your peers so often have the same vulnerabilities. You and your co-workers also have much in common because you were selected by the same person. You are all reflections of your boss's taste. Peers are as clearly defined a group, and with as many interests in common, as dog breeders, model railroad enthusiasts, or comptrollers. This is true whether you are talking about secretaries, operating managers, customer representatives, or auto mechanics. Peers share a view of the organization and of each other based on common experiences. Even one step up or down the corporate ladder will change the perspective.

Many of your co-workers may appear at first glance to be harmless; they may seem withdrawn from the competition for advancement or just more money. You have judged some of them to be "incompetent," though you may not have used that exact word. Many seem to be concentrating on their jobs and to be ducking office politics. They drink coffee at their desks and brown bag it for weeks at a time. Do not be misled. They have sensitive antennae which are constantly filtering the environment for storm warnings. Some are thinking up power games to play, possibly at your expense. Others may actually be plotting your political and professional demise. You need to turn those attitudes around before anyone takes action.

Power building with peers means influencing thinking and behavior, either by example or through relationships, or trading on a quid pro basis. Your peers have some, but not all, of the same needs and wants you have. What makes it so hard to trade power with them is that you and they are simultaneously both cooperative and competitive! Your relationship with your peers can never be entirely stable. You and they will compete more intensely at some times, less so at others, but you will always be competitors. Nothing can make you genuine friends.

Remember those departmental meetings during which all of you vied for the boss's attention? No one had anything monumental to say; everyone felt the need to say something strictly as a defensive measure. This is the most significant difference in power building with peers as opposed to power building with either your boss or your subordinates. Your peers will act defensively, even if it is not in their own best interests. Sometimes they will act to hurt or obstruct your interests even if they suffer at the same time. This means that you have to suspend your disbelief, when you find a peer doing something you judge to be career suicide, until you can investigate. Look for who, rather than what, is the target of this behavior. It may have been a defensive rather than a building move. It will almost always be a carefully calculated risk.

BUILDING INFLUENCE WITH PEERS

Do not try to measure your effectiveness at influence building by what your peers say about you. They are unlikely to acknowledge that you regularly influence them, espe-

cially if there is great competition among you. If they follow
your lead and negotiate with you, you have built power with
them. It is unlikely you will engage in visible power struggles with your peers. The less obvious your dealings the
better. It could make your boss very nervous to see all of
you dividing up power (possibly his or hers) at the water
cooler. Demanding that your peers feel a particular way will
cause you endless problems; ditto demanding they be sincere. That is why the social worker style is absolutely in-
appropriate here. How they feel is not important unless they
act out those feelings and you are hurt professionally in the
process. They are required only to fulfill their bargains.
Here are some of the best methods for influencing your
peers.

1. Information is as important to your peers as it is to
your boss, but your peers want a different kind of information than your boss does. Your office competitors are
usually plugged into the same grapevines you are. They are
hearing the same news from the same sources. Do not un-
derestimate what one unhappy peer can and will do to you
if provoked. Always assume that those at your level understand the informal system at least minimally—not perfectly,
but enough so they can use it if necessary.

2. Creating a trust relationship with peers can be a very
positive source of influence. For instance, while one supervisor might not appear promotable to management, he
or she may be very powerful among his/her peers. All the
other supervisors believe that this person has a direct line
to management's thought processes. They ask for and follow
this supervisor's advice, match their reactions to his, and
generally play follow-the-leader.

What is peculiar about this kind of influence is that peers

and management so pointedly disagree in their assessment. In theory, management's opinion should prevail. Those above the supervisors do not see the magic; therefore, in their view it does not or should not exist. Yet it does exist and will be influential. One usually finds this sort of peer power in nonprofit organizations because it rests on longevity, extra education, or expertise. People with Ph.D.s are often revered in nonprofit organizations other than universities, where Ph.D.s are the norm. In corporations the assumption is often made that the Ph.D. is odd. Why would he/she have taken the time to get that degree, especially if he/she is not going to teach? Corporate types do not often recognize the prestige of the Ph.D.

Longevity frequently buys trust. Peers assume that the person in question has survived because of his/her greater familiarity and expertise with the informal system. Knowing the long-term history of the organization can be valuable. And individual can use this information to assume power by training his/her peers and orienting them to the informal system, something never done through the chain of command. If done well, it creates dependencies. The trainees owe the trainer something, usually loyalty and future favors. There is a fine line between being a trainer and being an acculturator. Some of these people are really selling a party line, albeit rarely the official one, instead of being neutrally helpful. At first the trainee may buy the trainer's version of the facts. If the "facts" turn out to be nonfacts, it will cancel the relationship and negate any need to repay the help.

Object: to assume the role of expert using longevity, additional education, or expertise. You can advise and influence peers even when those above and below you on the chart cannot see why you have this power. In times of organizational instability the *expert*'s power will increase geometrically because he/she can interpret current news in light of the past.

3. Some people sell themselves to their peers as lifestyle experts-at-large or as popular role models. They gain power by dressing a little more stylishly, reading the new books first, and/or by consciously living and chronicling a trendy lifestyle. They may seem to be financially better off even though they are paid the same salary as others. They just spend money differently.

People still respond positively to those people they think are "popular." Popularity is always self-created. People are not forced to court or accept the esteem of others. The power thus created exists only with peers. Others in the hierarchy have their own influence leaders. There is no evidence of "universal" popularity within companies even though an occasional CEO will ask public relations to begin building such a legend in his behalf. People on other branches of the corporate tree have to do it for themselves. The person who gains power by being liked often helps along the attractions of personality by doing favors for people, giving advice, and generally making him/herself agreeable. There may or may not be physical attractiveness. Great beauty in a man or woman is often an obstacle to power because it arouses envy. It is certainly a barrier to being taken seriously. Consumer magazines have long since sold the public on the notion that beauty is hard work, that it interferes with a person's career.

Object: to use trendiness and/or an attractive personality to create power based on popularity. While this works very well in good times, it can boomerang in uncertain times. The next level up, always monitoring what the troops are up to, may assume that *popular* is a synonym for *unpro-*

ductive. Keeping relationships warm with those up the ladder is essential if you use this approach. If it has not been your style in the past to court popularity, you will find it more than ordinarily difficult to begin now.

You are not the only one with these tools. Inside the organization you and your peers start the race more or less as equals. Outside the organization is another story, which makes it possible to turn outside contacts into a competitive advantage.

THE ASSOCIATION CONNECTION

Many of your peers are not plugged into trade or professional association networks. If they are under thirty, they may not yet have discovered how valuable these networks can be. These professional groups may not have had college chapters or feeder groups or your peers may be only vaguely aware that such groups even exist. If your peers are over thirty, they may have told themselves that they do not need professional groups right now. Otherwise savvy people sometimes drop out of their trade or professional society once their careers seem to be established. Usually they let their membership lapse just before they have a desperate need for many strategically placed contacts. The result is that your peers have cut themselves off from rumors about your department or company that circulate within the informal systems of other companies. Since competitive companies have the greatest possible need for and interest in each other, this is an opportunity you can exploit to help you build power in your office.

If someone in your department had an idea for a service

or product, he or she would try to find out if a competitor had already tried it and whether it had been successful. If your boss were looking for a new job, it is reasonable that your company's competitors would know long before you heard it internally. If you are genuinely plugged into networks outside the company, you will find this a source of potential influence and trading power. Your diligence in research will be rewarded.

How and under what circumstances you share this information determines with whom you will associate. If you are new to the company, it affects who includes you at lunch; who seeks you out, albeit unwillingly; even how your boss evaluates you. Many bosses expect you to be an outside-the-company information gatherer and will reward you for regularly delivered rumors. Someone with a continuing source of fresh information can establish and maintain unlimited relationships both inside and outside the organization.

As you become known for accurate appraisals of events, based on personal shrewdness applied to information from your extensive network, you also begin to package ideas. This may start as you shape information of impending misfortune to pass on to a colleague in trouble. It may be in the way you temper the information you give to your boss. As time passes, people begin to accept your packaged version as fact. Of course it is fact, but you have given it a particular framework. You have fleshed it out. This helps you influence how others receive even very basic news. It may earn you a reputation for tact.

The possession of top-quality information can overcome your peers' prejudices. Many women deeply resent being frozen out by the "old boys." It is ego threatening and career damaging because the boys are exchanging information the women need and want. How to muscle in? Getting in was, and remains, a process of bringing something to the gathering. Why should the boys include women competitors— justice, fairness, rightness? That is silly and would not change the mind of one-tenth of one percent of adult males. Doesn't it seem far more likely that men would be willing to change their exclusionary policies if women brought something to the table that the men wanted but had difficulty getting personally? The possession of desirable information can help anyone to be included by groups from which he/she would surely be otherwise excluded. It changes the equation from dislike/like to worthless/valuable. It also changes the relative position of the outsider from supplicant to someone others are eager to cultivate.

Most people would consider news of job openings or potential openings in other companies valuable information. As you know, only the neediest and least-connected person would voluntarily go to a company's personnel department to inquire about job openings. The well-connected person would get the scoop at a trade or professional society meeting long before personnel in the company heard that an opening was about to occur. Most smart people over thirty who are not self-employed are perpetual job hunters, or at the very least job news hunters. This information has great value. If your peers know that you get job information first, they will approach you. They will also expect to give you something in return for this information.

Your company may keep its less savvy employees from knowing it is losing or has lost its competitive edge, but it is highly unlikely that your competitors won't sniff this out. If you are plugged into your competitors and you hear such news through your contacts, you could use it to buy yourself some thinking time. Thinking time equals time to plan. If the company is not yet publicly in trouble, you might be able to help yourself before the company's problems become known. You could trade those rumors to selected peers, if you choose, for information you need or want.

The perspective and interpretations of employees who have left the company is often worth a great deal. These people now have new bases for comparison. They can point out implications or reinterpret incidents which you have long since decided had no predictive value. They can see patterns. Companies often deliberately try to buy such perspectives when they pass over "homegrown" talent in favor of outsiders. You can find former employees to talk with just by asking the person with the most seniority for names of the most agreeable of the departed.

Why then, with so many obvious power building advantages, do so few people build information resources outside the organization? Because it is such very hard work! Imagine being endlessly and convincingly nice to people you could not possibly like! It requires consistent work to keep relationships warm and firm in order to get information every week, not just once a month at a group meeting. Who, other than the truly driven, would spend the time and energy? But consider this: Who would not want the information if someone else had already gathered it?

Information sharing with peers is dangerous unless you separate your personal gut reactions to the information from the facts you have uncovered. That is, you may pass on to a peer the news that your mutual boss has put her resume on the street but keep mum about what you think this means and what you plan to do if and when your boss leaves. Never share your plans or tactics with anyone, especially not with your peers. They will have no qualms about implementing what you said you planned to do, even if you accuse them of outright idea theft. After all, they might have thought of it anyway. How could you prove they did not?

Information sharing makes you powerful because others seek you out as a news source. You may have to share a few tidbits to let your peers know you have news, but do not give away free what you have worked so hard to get. Those who want to share the bounty must assist you in return. Many people try to put others hopelessly in their debt by doing multiple favors or by repeatedly sharing the most important and timely scoops. Don't. If too many people owe you favors, it is even worse than if no one does. Eventually they will begin to avoid you and exclude you from groups because they will feel that they cannot ever even the score. This is both embarrassing and demotivating. Everybody else is keeping a running score of who has helped or hurt them, and you should too.

Object: to use outside sources to gain internal influence. You trade information for inclusion in those groups you wish to be part of, or you trade information for other information. You use this information to establish yourself as a predicator of events and to broker power.

IDENTIFYING PREDATORS

Among us there are those who specialize in terrorist tactics. In any group of ten peers there will be at least one person who, while seeming to be on the outskirts, actually looks for opportunities to upset or create a dependency in others within the group. This is the dark side of information gathering.

A terrorist reaffirms bad news to the vulnerable. "I heard

your performance appraisal wasn't good this time. What are you going to do?" The terrorist then reverts to the role of adviser. "If you give me the details, I'll try to help." This is a manipulative technique to get the person, who the terrorist may only surmise is in trouble, to reveal far more than he or she should. What does it matter, the victim reasons. The terrorist seems to know almost the whole story anyway. The victim may also sense that he is being shunned by others who know he is in trouble and so welcome the attention, however predatory. Although it is a technique as old as history, it still works. People in trouble (or who think they are) frequently describe those troubles in great detail to peers, entirely against their own interests.

Terrorists expect to get information without having to work for it. They would rather manipulate than work for or share information. This tactic works only with peers because a boss or subordinate would not have the same kind of relationship with the terrorist and therefore would have no need to tolerate such behavior. Even a boss who is very insecure would still think that he should not confide in a subordinate, and a subordinate would be loathe to confide in a manager who controls his future. By creating an "us against the world" mentality, the terrorist gets what he or she wants rather efficiently. By getting the whole story about someone's trouble, the terrorist obtains the power to trade it with someone else for something he or she wants. Only when almost everyone in the group recognizes the game will the terrorist lose his or her power to extract information by engendering false comradeship in the victim.

Object: to identify and exclude terrorists from your own network. Terrorists are fundamentally lazy people who play on the fears of others. They are often careful observers and are shrewd at guessing the nature of a co-worker's problem and then insinuating that they already know the facts. The victim then reveals all of the details, however damaging, figuring it is already in the grapevine. The more upwardly mobile the people in a group, the more likely it is for one or more terrorists to lurk among them. You can, if you look carefully, identify and exclude these people from your own network. The definitive sign of a terrorist is that he/she is attracted only by problems. Terrorists skip the good news and the celebrations.

NEGOTIATING DEALS WITH PEERS

As with your boss, influencing peers has its limits. You may be respected and liked without being able to make that work for you when you need something specific or a particular piece of information. That is when you should negotiate.

Negotiating with peers is a much more open process than negotiating with a boss because there is no need to worry about protocol. You can barter for help, support, access to different sources within the grapevine, introductions to people outside the company who could help you within, and introductions to people within the company you could not otherwise meet easily or comfortably. In short, if a peer can do something for you, or you can bring up something that he/she might be able to do for you, it can be bartered for.

As in dealing with your boss, you always start with the grid. No two people at your level, however similar they may seem to be, have identical needs, desires, and interests. You must treat each as an unknown to be researched.

One caveat: These people are past, present, and/or future

competitors, not just in your present work arena but in others you might move to. If they are about your age, you could meet them ten, fifteen, or thirty years from now. Because they and you may have a long, if sporadic, association, never try to turn them into friends, especially if you plan to continue working in the same industry. You must maintain some emotional distance. It is impossible and unwise to form or maintain close, personal relationships with people who may be forced to rupture those relationships at some later date in order to hold on to a paycheck. Do not put yourself in the position of having to choose between the needs of a friend and your own career.

When you barter with your co-workers, what you ante up must always be something that you actually can deliver yourself and can afford to part with. You cannot afford to part with your private analyses of people or events which, should your analyses prove correct, would boost your career. You cannot afford to barter away good will. Remember that if you create an enemy, you will have that enemy virtually forever.

THE ACTUAL NEGOTIATION

With these constraints in mind, here is an example of negotiating with peers. You have a colleague, a supervisor like yourself, who is exceptionally good at divining which way top management's wind is blowing. He never knows what the information means, and he doesn't care. He is just good at analyzing. For months a rumor has been circulating that management plans a major reorganization of your department. Your boss will retain part of the department which is slated to be expanded from thirty to sixty people. One of the four supervisors will be named as the assistant manager for about twenty of the new people.

You want the job. Your co-worker wants it as much. He believes that his track record speaks for itself. (Nobody's ever does. It is always being interpreted and reinterpreted situationally.) He has been a supervisor for five years and has always received above average performance appraisals. Like most people, he is neither flawless nor a villain. His manner is often abrasive, and he loves to pull rank. Although the people who work for him respect him, they do not really like him. Turnover in his area is higher than the departmental average but not so high as to cause him a political problem.

He holds the one piece of information that you need to plan your campaign for the job: He knows top management's timetable. His father is a golfing pal of the chairman of the board. It is not in your co-worker's best interests to tell you when the reorganization is going to take place as you would then be able to plan a campaign to influence the right people. However, he does need a piece of information you have, which you both know he cannot get from top management. He does not have any fix on what the grapevine says about him at an operational level, that is, at the higher levels of middle management. He is not alone. How many people pursue information which they are not sure will be palatable? You can supply that missing link. You can show him a mirror image. (Needless to say you would do this with scrupulous integrity and careful documentation, while protecting your sources. This is dynamite!)

Look at the grid in order to shape these negotiations. Your co-worker wants a summary of his image. You want a timetable. Are those two pieces of information equal or nearly equal in value? Who knows? There is no outside source to judge. How important to you is the piece of information you want? How important is it to your colleague?

I WANT	I (CAN) GIVE
HE/SHE WANTS	HE/SHE (CAN) GIVE

Can another person trade you the information you want? Would this be less risky than a review of your co-workers's image with all the possibilities of hurt feelings and misunderstanding? How highly does your co-worker value the feedback you can give? Are there other peers able and willing to give the same sort of information? If not, the information you have may be worth two pieces of information from him.

The value of information is always enhanced or damaged by the credibility of the source, the immediacy of the information (today is better than last week), and its ultimate usefulness to the hearer. News that can cause people to change strategies or behavior is very valuable.

If you are put off by the evaluating and trading of information in this way, you cannot be seriously interested in power. What could power be in an office situation but access to, or exclusion from, information? If no one believes you have information which they lack access to and that they can only gain through a trade, you will not be powerful. This is true at every level from top management to file clerk.

I WANT	I (CAN) GIVE
Top management's timetable	Image assessment
HE/SHE WANTS	HE/SHE (CAN) GIVE
Image assessment	Top management's timetable

Before you approach your peer you need to prepare a grid just like the one you prepared for your boss. List the items you can trade and those you think will interest him.

Your approach to negotiate with him should be simple and direct. You say, "Let's have coffee [or a drink after work]. I'd like to talk to you." This lets him know it is a private and presumably a serious discussion. He will not bring his squash buddies. You open the discussion by recognizing both the mutuality of your interests and the essential competitiveness of your relationship. Never suggest to a direct competitor that you think the relationship is stronger or more personal than the need each of you has to compete or excel. If your competitor is reasonably savvy, he will think you do not understand the issues at all or do not grasp what is happening. It may make him feel guilty because he does not feel the same warmth or concern for you. These attitudes will hinder the business you want to conduct. Say, "I think you and I have an interest in common. I'm interested in knowing when you think the reorganization will take place. I know you've expressed some concern about middle management's feelings about you and your work. How about a trade?"

Your colleague can do one of two things. He can say, "Sure, here's what I think is happening," or he can say, "I don't know. Are you sure that's a good idea? After all, we're both in the running for the assistant manager's job." If he says the latter, he is signaling you that he does not think the information you propose to trade is of equal value. At this point go to the second item on your list of possible needs and say, "Are you interested in who is writing the job description for the new position?" If he says, "Yes, that would be good to know," you've got a deal.

Obviously, both of you are anteing up a certain amount of trust as well as information. If you find your co-worker has lied to you or deliberately colored reality, no possibility for cooperation between you will exist. If you color your information, the same is true. That is a powerful incentive to keep the facts sharply separated from any political fantasy.

Another example would be the trading of a good job lead for the information you want. In every competitive situation a job lead in one's pocket is often more comforting and stress reducing than a pitcher of martinis. The job lead must be very fresh as you will not be able to keep that type of news quiet long.

WHY PEER NEGOTIATIONS FAIL

Occasionally you do everything right, and you still cannot come to a mutually beneficial arrangement with a co-worker. You know you have hit an area of warm interest; you can tell the person wants what you are offering. What prevents a deal from being struck?

1. You have misjudged your co-workers's depth of feeling on an issue. For instance, you believe you have offered a suitable trade. Your co-worker believes that, even so, the information you seek has far greater value to you than what you have offered has to him. He is assuming an essentially defensive position. It is no longer a game of giving to get, it is a game of keeping you from doing something you want to do.

The best way to handle this is to treat it as a deadlock. Assume that multiple rephrasings of what is involved will help break the deadlock and get things back on track. Don't say, "Hey, you're just throwing up roadblocks," even if that is obvious. Always try to demonstrate several different ways in which your co-worker's interests are being served. In a deadlock the ability to sell is vital.

2. Your co-worker dislikes you more personally or professionally than she wants what you are offering. If she fails, it won't be so painful if you fail alongside her. When you sense there is personal hostility involved, emphasize that while you are happy to do business with her, there are always other resources. She is not your only source. This will quickly give you a reading on how serious she is about cutting a deal. It will also allow you to test the depth of her hostility against the possibilities of future dealings. If it is a very deep hostility, you will want to try to neutralize her influence while cultivating alternative sources. Don't use deductive reasoning to analyze the situation. There may be no particular reason why she dislikes you; she just does.

3. Your co-worker fears your success more than his own failure. For example, if you succeed in getting the supervisory job, you are not as likely to give this co-worker the special attention he gets from the boss. His greatest fear is that his influence will be forcibly diminished. Do not raise this as an issue. Suggest instead that you are willing to deal with him now and will always be ready to do so in the future. That ought to be your position anyway, so go public with it now!

4. Some other co-worker has been influencing the person with whom you are trying to trade. This influence need not have been in the form of negative remarks about you. What is likely is that the co-worker pointed out very clearly how you would benefit from a particular action or piece of information. Now your negotiating partner is rethinking her

position in light of new information. That is one reason why
it is especially helpful to do your negotiating in one session
and end the deal as quickly as possible. If it takes three
different sessions and there is still no clear decision, find
another trading partner.

5. Your peer reneges because he decides that embarrassing you would be more fun than fulfilling his agreement.
This can only happen if you agree to be embarrassed. Remember, everything you have done and everything you have
attempted to do went through the informal system. All your
negotiations were oral; nothing was on paper. For you to
be embarrassed would require your peer to produce something tangible that others could see. The incident, as it
occurred, is much too long to relate in sufficient detail to
give others a sense of why you ought to be embarrassed.
In this type of situation you would do best to cut your peer
out of the networks you control and then keep quiet. Let
him talk himself into something that will embarrass him as
he tries to talk himself out of it.

Do not worry about getting too far ahead of your peers.
Your peers will not mind your rise in influence and power
as long as you continue to work through the informal system.
It is a myth to suppose they are all equally ambitious. A
majority may be elsewhere mentally and not particularly
anxious to work as hard as they see you are doing. Still,
they do not want you to get too far ahead. It pays to down-
play your successes, especially with sensitive peers, and
always to share the credit, whether it is precisely deserved
or not. You are still building; you have not arrived.

Your peers respond more to change itself than to the
actual content of change. They need to be reassured at all
times that you are thinking and working in small bits, not

coups d'état. Organizations, even the most innovative, high technology ones, are internally and structurally conservative, and you must respect the culture.

Now that you know how to build the right kind of relationships with your peers, it is time to work on your subordinates.

7. INFLUENCING YOUR SUBORDINATES

SYL Parkerton, M.D., inherited a secretary when he became chairman of the department of internal medicine at the hospital. Joyce had been there twenty years. She knew everyone on staff and had seen four chairmen arrive full of reformist's zeal, only to depart a few years later having accomplished little. Syl had two options: He could try to document poor performance on Joyce's part and have her fired or transferred, or he could try to get her to play on his team. Fearing an age discrimination suit, the personnel department resisted any attempt to fire Joyce. Syl decided he really had only one option. He began to seek information about Joyce. He learned she had been single for five years following a very messy divorce from a physician. The other physicians, while not anxious to introduce her to any prospective husbands, nonetheless believed her husband had been a cad and felt inclined to protect her interests. Syl's plan as it evolved was actually a plot to either raise Joyce's ambition or find her a husband who would insist she leave the job. What made him a power builder rather than a manipulator was that he directly negotiated with Joyce, taking her ideas and feelings into account. He tried to influence her to seek a higher paying, more prestigious job within the hospital. In exchange for some political advice on the chairman of another department, he introduced her to some physician friends in the hospital he had left. Within six months the two of them were working as a team. Joyce eased his transition into the job by giving guided tours to all buried bodies and landmines. She sang his praises in the grapevine, causing Syl's colleagues to conclude in some cases that theirs was more than a professional relationship. It was not. Joyce considers him the best chairman she has ever worked for. Their relationship is such that when he moves on, she will too, benefiting everyone, including whoever succeeds Syl as chairman.

Sometimes a manager looks over his or her subordinates and feels like Luke Skywalker in the bar scene from *Star Wars*. Where did those quarrelsome losers come from? It is hardly comforting to know you personally selected them from a rather large universe. Even less so to think you recruited them in what you believed was your own image and self-interest. Still, as long as you have them, you might as well involve them in your power building strategies. They can help you in many ways, provided you teach them why it is in their best interests to do so.

Subordinates make excellent sounding boards, especially for schemes you would hesitate to let your peers hear about because these schemes are still in the incubation stage. For example, if you are planning to change your department's computer user policy, your subordinates can help you package the new policy by telling you what their experiences have been with the present policy. Do not expect them to volunteer this information or strive to have some input; this rarely happens. Their advice must be solicited.

Your subordinates can be excellent information exchangers. They can extend both your internal and external information networks by networking with those you have no time for or access to. They can put information which you want specific people to hear into the grapevine and thus increase your power by extending your influence.

Ultimately subordinates should be a source of upward thrust. If you have five superbly qualified, perfectly groomed candidates for your job standing by, the company must promote you. Otherwise that talent is likely to leave.

PERSUADING THE TROOPS

The unsophisticated manager might assume that, in most organizations, paycheck power is enough to cause subordinates to do anything the manager wants. If his subordinates do not cooperate, he can cut them off. He also has protocol and the formal system to fall back on, and that should be worth something. Why influence them—much less negotiate with them? Although fear for one's job will keep the desperate or weak-minded in line temporarily, over time these managerial tactics often backfire.

Subordinates may take up malicious compliance with enthusiasm, doing only what they are ordered to do and refusing to think. They will spend every spare moment reading their job descriptions to make sure they are not doing anything not mandated to them. High achievers, on whom most managers' reputations ultimately depend, are rarely if ever impressed with terror tactics. They have enough confidence to believe they would be better treated elsewhere—and to act on that belief. Probably the best reason not to use fear as a motivator is purely pragmatic. There are easier, less risky ways to get the troops to do things your way. If you use these better methods, management above you will attribute your success with your subordinates to superior management skill, which you will in fact have developed.

Subordinates long to see their own "Rules of the Organization" carved in stone. They long for enough power to protect and enhance their positions. They need some feeling of control over their work lives. They are not notably loyal unless they like the boss personally. Quite often they do not like the boss; at least not when the boss wants them to. If you do not want to work at being likeable and at establishing personal connections with your people (surely a mind-numbing task), you will need to use influence and negotiation. In order to do this you need to know what your subordinates want most and what they will respond to.

WHAT SUBORDINATES REALLY WANT

Your subordiniates are most likely to respond enthusiastically to two things: on-the-job coaching in transferable skills and truthful, detailed explanations of how things work. Even the slowest-witted subordinate has deciphered the proliferating clues that job security is not what it used to be. Promises of "we're all just family here" or "we never fire anyone who has proven him/herself" no longer impress them. Many are beginning to suspect that job security no longer exists in any organization, including the government. The 1980s is the age of Paladin, "Have Gun, Will Travel." Therefore, subordinates employ different criteria than they have used in the past in judging a "good" boss versus a "bad" boss. The most important characteristic in a "good" boss is one who coaches rather than commands.

Modeling far exceeds command as an effective management technique. Modeling is a combination of actually showing someone how to do something and then providing feedback as the person attempts to repeat the action. The best use of this method is in teaching people how to handle people problems in a certain way or to approach complex problems with a particular style. It is a very important tool to shorten someone's learning curve. A manager who can provide coaching and who can also be a role model does not need to send a subordinate to a training seminar. If you provide modeling, not just in learning the job but in adapting to changes in it, your subordinates will help convince others you are powerful. They will shape the stories they put into the grapevine to showcase your best qualities.

Why do you need to be seen as a powerful boss instead of just a good one? In all our conversations with clients about bosses, one idea stands out: The good manager is powerful while the bad manager is weak. Subordinates often see events as outlines. Rarely do they understand the nuances. A weak manager invariably is one who seems buffeted by events rather than in control of them. The weak manager relies heavily on the formal system. Most important, to be seen as powerful enhances power. Your boss and peers will also be influenced by what your subordinates think.

Why wouldn't your subordinates play down your good qualities or try to sabotage you? Ultimately it is not in their best interests to do so. As long as they are learning from you, polishing skills they can take to the next job, the bright ones will support you. The weaker ones might want to sabotage you because you press them for ever-increasing productivity; however, they lack the brain power and aggression to undermine you without help from the bright ones on whom you have already got a lock.

In addition, knowledge about how the system really works at their level is very important to subordinates. They are often confused by the subtle differences between the formal and informal systems. For instance, a manager is fired for "pressing his boss too hard." Your people have heard this through the grapevine, but they really do not understand what it means. How did the manager press? Did his boss overreact? It chills your people to hear of patently political firings with no "official" parameters. If you can offer even a bit more unofficial explanation, they will respond positively. In most cases these explanations will apply to other work situations as well.

There are other things your subordinates want almost as much as coaching and "how things work" information. Instead of turning off when the office grapevine carries the usual litany of complaints, listen carefully. The grapevine is not just "idle" gossip but important information you can turn into capital with subordinates. Every gripe is an unmet need, and many gripes are about things you can easily change or use as bargaining chips with others. Here are some of them.

1. "There are always unpleasant surprises here." Subordinates everywhere complain about the cavalier way management keeps them off balance. Who knows what is going

on? Everything that happens surprises someone. Rarely do managers merchandise motives down the ladder as effectively as they might. Your subordinates want to know how and what top management really thinks. They will report to their networking associates that you are a guru just because you share this type of information with them. Why are you hoarding such structural data when it can buy you so much informal power with the troops? Knowing how things are really done, how decisions are really made, takes away some of their sense of insecurity.

For example, an almost universal management failing is a desire to keep the troops from getting too much "why" information. Managers love to hoard information about the mechanics of decision making. Normally gregarious vice-presidents are often mute before subordinates who ask simple "why" questions. They fear an argument, a loss of face or authority, or simply resent being asked. It would be to your advantage as a manager to let the lowest-ranked employee question why particular decisions were made. You would learn something about their perceptions that would help you package decisions to them the next time. The employees would certainly feel a greater investment in the execution of whatever decision is made. Answering questions is never the equivalent of abdicating the right to make the decision, and it does build influence.

Objects: to turn a thirst for detail and explanation into power; to use information your subordinates cannot easily get to build power with and through them; to create a feeling that you do have access to more power, thereby making it so; to create a channel for subordinates to question decisions so they can be persuaded to buy in.

2. "Management does not reward us for the news." Do you reward your subordinates for information? If you do

not, you should. If they know that you want the hottest rumors, the insane as well as the reasonable, they will deliver. However, if you ever punish someone for bad news, you will forever lose access to the information your subordinates can provide. If you show any sign of shock, dismay, or anger when you hear a rumor, you have "punished" the person who brought it.

Your subordinates connect at different levels in the company. They eat and talk with different people and have a different perspective on the company than you do. Their formal job descriptions do not suggest in any way that they are to keep you supplied with informal news. If you want that news (and you should because it enhances your trading relationships up), you have to maintain the most amicable relationships possible with your subordinates. Practice enthusiastic inscrutability. It will buy you an endless stream of tradeable information.

Objects: to increase your research through your subordinates; to use their search for information and their networking as an extension of your own; to increase their sense of participation and reward them for information. This is where you get the information which you can trade both vertically and horizontally.

3. "Management is unfair." Fairness is a burning issue at the bottom of the ladder. Many managers choose to ignore this thirst for justice because they assume that subordinates overreact. They reason that if they ignore this overreaction, it will somehow dissipate. It can be a fatal assumption. Subordinate dissatisfaction will temporarily go underground only to resurface later as sabotage. Giving the appearance of fairness and evenhandedness is a source of power because arbitrariness is so much easier and more fun, and everyone knows it! Managers who delight in "keeping the troops

guessing" should regularly do a sum on what that costs them in terms of power with their subordinates. For most people fair means logical. If there is no logical explanation for events, or any reason at all, the troops will assume the decision was unfair. Someone was being done in or done to.

There is no question that your subordinates can and will sabotage you if you give them reason to do so. If you answer their need for fairness in decision making, you actually change nothing but you buy some good will, which translates into influence. Your boss expects you to take the blame with your troops for his decisions, just as he takes the blame for some of the things you decide. Do it. Your subordinates also see this as a fairness issue. If you try to pass the buck back up, it undercuts your heroic stance and your partnership with them. Besides, it is too radical a departure from the protocol inherent in the chain of command.

Objects: to appear fair, whatever the facts; to acknowledge that your subordinates' desire for fairness, while troublesome, is legitimate and must be satisfied; to assume your share of the blame for company policy decisions.

4. "Nobody appreciates the work we do." Your subordinates want lavish, sustained recognition and appreciation. A major gripe everywhere is lack of appreciation. The more menial the job, the more this holds true. Most managers, if only subconsciously, operate on the theory that if things are going well, nothing need be said.

You have heard for years that recognition and appreciation motivate people. It is still true. Why, then, is it so hard to recognize and appreciate what people do? Lurking in the back of most managers' minds is one unworthy thought: "It shouldn't be this way. These people shouldn't need to be praised for showing up on time and doing the job. We're paying them." That is as true as it is irrelevant. If you are going to be standard bearers in your cause, they are going to have to be appreciated ad nauseam, recognized beyond reason. Otherwise, what possible incentive is there for them to work harder with greater attention to detail?

If you are going to use recognition and appreciation as rewards, it has to be done in public; no more writing letters for people's personal files or talking about your trusted associate only to your boss. People want to hear their names covered with praise in the grapevine. They want peers to say, "Hey, I hear the project you worked on went really well!" That is the recognition that means something. Even better are articles in the company newsletter, recognition plaques in public areas, and being mentioned in front of other employees. Who would not respond to such techniques? Recognition can never be overdone, but it must appear to be sincere. Do not give it formally and then take it back through the grapevine. If you are cynically stroking someone, it is not recognition and will not pass for such.

Praise sporadically but frequently. If a subordinate is having a particularly difficult time but is overcoming the difficulties, say something then. Do not wait until a long project is finished. Praise people for either not having made mistakes or for preventing them, as well as for correcting them. Do not be stingy. Most people have an insatiable desire for this kind of feedback. Do not limit your efforts to your own people. Praise anyone who is performing well, whomever they may report to.

Object: to use public recognition and praise in order to influence your employees. Being known as an appreciative boss will not hurt you anywhere in the hierarchy. Public opinion is as important there as it is in the world at large. Remember, good is not the opposite of demanding. Recognition and praise strengthen, not weaken, your hold on your people and their performance.

5. "Nothing ever happens here," the rank and file say. Subordinates want regular but controlled change. At this level change equals excitement. While you do not need to create circuses in the employee lounge, you do need to plan to move people regularly and see that they are learning new skills. This will improve productivity. Conversely, don't ever let a subordinate get a hammerlock on a particular job. The longer one individual is in a job, the more power he or she gathers. In some companies, subordinates have been allowed to hold jobs for so long that if they left it would take months to sort out what had been done and how. They fail to keep records because it is all in their memories. Besides, subordinates are not stupid. They know they are less likely to be fired or laid off if their departure would seriously inconvenience the boss. This is real power. Move now to short-circuit this kind of power within your area. You need not announce your reasons, just your intent to get everyone involved in learning new skills. Call it cross-training or, if you want more jargon, cross-functional job rotation.

Reward those subordinates who provide ideas for productivity increasing change, including restructuring jobs. Let people know that no assignment is permanent. If they are not delighted with the current assignment, they may like the next one better. This will cut turnover, if that is what you want to do, by showing people that they do not have to move out of the department in order to grow and learn.

Objects: to build influence by keeping people on the move; to prevent subordinates from building power by establishing exclusive control over a particular function, or job; to cut turnover by regularly providing "new jobs."

NEGOTIATING WITH YOUR SUBORDINATES

Even though you may influence your employees on an ongoing basis, there are times when you will need to negotiate with them. Let's say that there is something outside the normal range of duties that is important to you. You want your subordinates to do this new task willingly and in a particular way. You could order them to do it, but this can be risky, since you want them to think while they work. Suppose you wanted your people to do something in a particular way that required far greater effort than would ordinarily be necessary. Finally, suppose you wanted your subordinates to invest themselves to a greater extent in their jobs. Instead of just going through the motions, it is important for each of them to think of him/herself as responsible for the success of the project. In each case you would have to negotiate for that service.

If an employee is not doing the ordinary, required job satisfactorily, you do not negotiate, you retrain or discipline. You should only use negotiation as a tool when you want something so badly that you are willing to give the subordinate something extra in order to obtain it, or if you want someone to execute a particular task without alteration or embellishment.

In order to negotiate, start with the same grid and the same techniques you used with your boss and your peers. You must define what you want in detail and what you will trade to get it.

Here is a practical example. A supervisor in a rehabilitation hospital had twelve social workers on her staff. Each was responsible for working with about ten patients daily. The patients were para- and quadriplegics, mostly swimming and automobile accident victims. One day it occurred to her that the patients needed a more active kind of cheering up than they were getting.

She called her staff together and proposed that each social worker make it his/her duty to cause each patient to smile daily. She said, "When I follow you down the hall, I want to see the patient you've just visited smiling when I look into the room." This was dubbed the Grin Campaign. The social workers were not noticeably enthused, but no one pointed out that this was not part of the job. They treated the Grin Campaign as a suggestion, not as an order. The patients did not smile more frequently than in the past, and it was obvious that the social workers saw this as a temporary management aberration.

The supervisor persisted. About half the staff then talked to patients, saying, "Look, do me a favor. When you see my supervisor, smile." The supervisor went back to the drawing board. Obviously her instructions were being breached. How could she get the social workers to carry them out? Performance appraisals were six months away. There was a freeze on salary increases, so there was little hope of either revenge or reward within the formal system. If she was to save the Grin Campaign, she needed a new tool. She decided to negotiate with them individually.

Here is what she did. She drew a negotiating grid for each staff member, using her knowledge of the individual to think up some reward that each might want. (The key to successful negotiation is to promise only those things which you personally deliver.) She compiled the overall list on page 154 of things she could do for them by herself.

Then she initiated one-on-one meetings with her staff.

She talked to Jack first. Here is what she said: "I want to discuss the Grin Campaign with you. I think this campaign is very important to the patients. I know some of the staff do not agree. If you'll agree to work at it—and I don't care how you do it as long as you get the desired result—I'll spend several hours next month helping you learn more about staff supervision." Jack had no interest in learning any supervisory skills. She tried again. He was interested in picking his own patients. He also warmed up to the idea of a general restructuring of the patient load, with input from everybody. A deal was cut.

She did this with each of the social workers and found that only two wanted the same things. Each of the others had a different need. Notice that no money or money equivalent, such as time off, was involved. The two who chose the same things were two people who wanted closer parking spaces. In the end, she kept the Grin Campaign going for six months. At this point she was convinced that it really did not make a significant difference in patient attitude or recovery, so she dropped it. Since her social workers were attached to their perks, she called each one in and renegotiated for something else that each could do.

Another manager in the same hospital sought to motivate the housekeeping staff. Their jobs were very routine and were often pressured and lonely; however, they were vital to the mission of the institution. With a staff of sixty people it was impossible for him or any one person to know each of these people well enough to negotiate easily with them as individuals. He taught his supervisors negotiation techniques and then negotiated with each of them to negotiate with their subordinates. The rest of the managers cannot understand how and why these two colleagues get greater productivity and cooperation out of their people for the very

I WANT	I CAN
	Give more public recognition through the grapevine
	Teach a supervisory skill which could be used in a higher level job
	Give more responsibility for his/her work
	Allow greater input on scheduling
	Give more time with the supervisor
	Restructure the patient load
	Arrange an opportunity to bid on new patients coming into the department
	Rotate the assignment of present patients
	Give parking space closer to the building. (She could control this, which was unusual.)
	Inaugurate a new system for giving immediate feedback on performance
	Give a chance to learn more about the informal system within the hospital
	Give a challenging new task or assignment
	Give access to supervisors in other hospitals who might hire social workers
SHE WANTS	SHE CAN GIVE

same money. They do not understand why these two managers are so visibly influential and so well thought of, when they seem to be doing the same thing as the other managers.

This technique works even better in a for-profit environment. For example, your secretary is in the terminal stages of inertia. She is doing very little because she feels inadequtely paid. You will be shocked to learn how many unmet needs besides money she has and how eager she is for those needs to be met. Negotiate with her and watch her performance improve.

This negotiating technique works with any kind of subordinate and can be taught to others. It rests on one primary assumption: No one's work-related needs are ever entirely met. Therefore, rather than thinking of money as the only means to motivate someone, it is more effective to look at psychic rewards. It makes the manager more effective and causes him/her to stand out from his/her competitors. Otherwise, the manager is left with nothing but money or fear; that can be fatal.

ADDITIONAL TIPS ON NEGOTIATING WITH SUBORDINATES

1. Do not attempt to use your formal power and negotiating techniques at the same time. That is, you must never say to an employee who has rejected an offer, "You really should take that." The process of negotiating must be as equal as you can possibly make it. Otherwise you are in the same trap as someone who must command. If the employee does not freely choose what you are offering, you cannot force the issue. The person who feels forced never gives you the specific performances you want. You will end up with someone who is only grudgingly going along with you.

2. Expect your peers to ask what you are doing to get such improved performances and increased loyalty from your troops. Explain the process. Just because you tell people how something is done does not mean that they will do it. Many companies send managers to formal courses on

how to negotiate. Do they apply these principles once they are back on the job? Rarely, because it requires at least twenty percent more effort on the manager's part to do so. Some people also feel threatened by even momentary equality between boss and subordinate. Somehow it diminishes the pleasure they get from playing a managerial role.

3. Expect that if you negotiate well and your people work more effectively, those above you in the chain of command may occasionally feel threatened by or hostile toward you. It is not easy to watch a subordinate do something effectively that you cannot or are not willing to do. As long as you act quietly, so that no official notice is taken of your efforts, you can have tremendous influence through the informal system. If the company newsletter wants to cover your efforts, decline unless you would like publicity as an entrée to a division you cannot physically reach. The important people will know what is going on.

WHEN NEGOTIATIONS WITH SUBORDINATES FAIL

Your subordinates will prove a ready audience for your efforts except in five instances. If any of these occur, you should take it very seriously. More than your relationship with your subordinate is threatened; your job may be on the line.

1. Your subordinates will not negotiate if they believe you are about to be fired or outplaced and hence you will not be present to fulfill any promises you make. If your subordinates seem very reluctant to get involved in any kind of performance-for-opportunity negotiations, they are telling you as clearly as they can, without saying the words,

that something or someone is threatening your job tenure. You must treat this as extremely threatening and begin to investigate immediately. Only something very grave would cause them to risk your displeasure. This is even truer if you have negotiated successfully with them in the past.

Do not ask them directly what is causing the problem. That will put them on the spot, and it is highly unlikely that even the most honest and supportive subordinate is going to give you the grim news. The person to check with is a peer who has access to the widest sources in the grapevine, preferably different sources from those you regularly network with. If the rumor is false, and you can see how and why it developed, confront the source and correct the informal record. If you do not, the prophecy may become self-fulfilling.

2. You and your boss are locked in a power struggle. It is so serious your subordinates believe that even if you win your performance will be impaired. You will not be fired, just reduced to political impotence. If they contract for any help from you, they are not sure you will be able to provide it. If their fears are justified, do not try to negotiate anything long-term. That means you will have to work very creatively with a very short list of things you can do for them immediately.

It is always possible that while you and your boss may be at odds, the gravity of the conflict has been exaggerated, especially if words have been exchanged. If that is the case, the only way your people will believe the truth is if you explain why, though serious, this conflict is not going to be fatal to your effectiveness or tenure.

3. You and a subordinate have a rivalry which is so intense that the subordinate refuses to act in his/her self-interest. Whatever started the rivalry has actually warped his/her

judgment and may also have altered yours. This has permanently ruptured any trust relationship which may have existed and prevents its reestablishment. This occurs most often when you are promoted from within and a vanquished peer lingers. You and an employee may have been at odds over job responsibilities. Your subordinate is constantly trying to enlarge his job at the expense of his peers. He has made several people angry but never so angry that you felt the need to confront him, much less fire him. It has been annoying and bears watching. His desire to do everything just as he wishes, regardless of the effect on others, makes him unwilling to negotiate with you. If you two struck a deal, it would lock him in and benefit you both.

4. Your employee is so stressed and burned out that nothing you can say will make a difference. This often happens in hospitals with nurses, interns, and others in very high-stress situations. These people are so overextended emotionally there is no way for them to give even one ounce more. They may even have developed psychological problems that prevent them from being reliable trading partners.

It is difficult for managers to diagnose burnout. Often the person who will not negotiate, or once having agreed to something will not fulfill his agreement, seems either indifferent or just maliciously resistant. The way to tell if it is really burnout is to see how the person behaves after work. Burnout victims tend to take their malaise home with them and to withdraw from social contact with other workers. The malicious register tends to brighten up after five.

5. The employee has had such bad experiences with the company recently, possibly because of the economic situation, that he/she has no desire to do anything but hold on until he/she finds a new job. This is an almost infallible tip-off that the employee is merely marking time until he/she

departs. If pressed too hard, the employee may agree to something that he/she knows will not be fulfilled because he/she will be gone soon.

Trust your instincts when working with your subordinates. If they perform for you, it indicates a high level of trust in your integrity and a vote of confidence in your future with the organization.

All negotiations will be ongoing, as your priorities, needs, and wants change. Your subordinates will get with the program once they see the effect and will finally initiate trades with you. Encourage them in this and watch your reputation for effectiveness grow.

8. POWER BUILDING BY INDUSTRY

IMAGINE that you are looking at the whole spectrum of employers in the United States and are trying to decide exactly which one, or which of several, would offer you the best opportunities for maximizing your talents. It is a nearly impossible task. Even if you could do the research and still work at your present job, you would have all of the problems of verification we have already talked about. It would take a tremendous amount of time. If you are changing careers (that is, you are going to use a different set of skills on your next job) or if you are just changing work theaters (that is, you will use your current skills in a different kind of business or industry), you will benefit from these industry power guidelines. After all, changing directions is always a risk. Why not minimize as much of this risk as possible? To get the most from these capsules keep the following provisos in mind.

These guidelines are intended for people with a minimum

of five years' work experience. However, even if you are twenty-two years old and looking for your first full-time job, this information may help you make an initial choice. Either way you would benefit from this hard-boiled view of the work world.

No one characteristic of any industry should be definitive in your choice of either an industry or a particular organization within it. If you decide that your personality and style fit banking better than accounting, and you have the skills for both, you should use other indicators. Principal among them would be how important your skills are to the bottom line profit and loss in each industry. For example, the position of auditor in a CPA firm is a line job; in a bank it is a staff job. If you are an auditor and primarily interested in power building and increased income, a public accounting firm should be your first choice. Bank auditors, although important, are strictly staff people. They have internal, but it is unlikely that one will become CEO unless he or she combines this experience with work in a line area. If you do not desire the greater stress and income of public accounting, working as a bank auditor would be an ideal choice. Banks will always have them.

Your gut-level instincts should always triumph in this decision-making process. If your instinct tells you that public accounting would stylistically fit your needs but you really dislike using accounting skills, then skip it. It is time to go back to the drawing board. A person with "interests" or "talents" can never compete with people of passion. Unless you think accounting is the most fascinating industry in the world, you can never have enough talent to get a partnership in any public accounting firm. Owners and partners of these firms are quite adept at separating the merely talented from the emotionally committed.

As with every kind of data, there will always be rare exceptions to the standard profiles. There are accounting firms run by people with creative, freewheeling styles just as there are advertising firms in the clutches of accountants or people with highly linear styles. These exceptions make it imperative for you to always verify what you think you know. If you find a firm whose style is vastly different from the profiles here, ask questions. Why? There should be an explanation. It may not be logical, but it exists and you need to know what it is.

If you find large numbers of people in any company who are very different from the typical industry profile, then look for a top management that has been recently appointed, is reorganizing, or is changing in response to market conditions. It is possible to identify typical industry power profiles because certain jobs attract and hold certain personality types and certain work styles. The people who succeed in specific industries are those who work best within that unique culture.

For example, a newspaper reporter with no reverence for the facts would not last long in an organization that worshiped the verifiable fact (or said it did). The fact enhancer might use this misplaced creativity in a very successful career as a novelist. There is no dishonest intent. Absolute verifiability is not as important to the novelist as to the reporter. If facts are not important to the reporters, editors, or publishers in a company, there is something wrong with the organization. It is deviating too far from the norms of its industry. You will not be able to build power in such an organization because it is not true to its type; survival is threatened.

POWER DIFFERENCES BETWEEN INDUSTRIES

We are going to look at three broad divisions of organizations: service businesses and nonprofit service organizations, including all branches of the government;
manufacturing businesses, including all of the combined
manufacturing/service organizations; and separately—because they are very different in terms of power building—
the so-called glamour industries. We are not interested in
how economists classify businesses. Many classify retailing
as a separate category whereas we have classed it with the
service businesses. We do this because we are primarily
interested in how power is acquired, maintained and used,
not in how the organization is structured economically.

Let us look broadly at these divisions. Each division
shares some characteristics with the others, but each also has some unique qualities. If you compare service and
manufacturing businesses, you will immediately see that
building and maintaining relationships, both within the
organization and with clients, is far more important in service businesses. A manufacturer may make a product that
is so far superior to its competitors' that customers will rush
to buy it. The product may not even be price sensitive; the
company can charge as much as it wants to because it has
no real competition. If another manufacturer subsequently
sells a better product, even if the original manufacturer's
sales people have built warm, wonderful relationships with
their customers, the customers will buy from the competition
regardless of their personal feelings. Their prior relationships will not affect the decision to buy a better product. If

the product is price sensitive, customers will switch to the cheapest manufacturer as long as quality and usefulness are not affected. If the price and product are identical, then relationships become important.

Glamour industries are more like service businesses. The glamour industries include the media (newspapers, television, magazines, radio, and publishing), advertising, movies, theater, music, dance, and public relations. Sales, although sometimes seen as glamorous, is not a glamour industry. Glamour does not necessarily mean money or prestige; it is much more a state of mind ratified by public recognition. It is possible to labor anonymously, even as president of the company, in manufacturing. In glamorous businesses the people, such as William S. Paley of CBS or Henry Luce of Time, Inc., are not anonymous. Part of the glamour is the fame.

SERVICE INDUSTRY PROFILES

Service businesses, which employ about thirty percent of the work force as we have previously pointed out, lack any reliable method for measuring results or objectively evaluating performance. No matter what the service is, it is difficult to separate it from the people who ultimately deliver it. For example, does a patient get well more quickly when treated by a warm, enthusiastic physician than when treated by a dour, indifferent one? Does the outgoing, articulate lawyer give better legal advice than the Sam Spade lookalike?

Some service businesses, notably banking, law, management consulting, and accounting, claim they do produce measurable results separated from the person delivering the service. This claim is arguable unless you believe that keeping the client happy is the measurable result. It is essential and desirable, but trying to measure why a client stays with a firm is difficult, particularly when most clients, when pressed for an opinion, will say, "I like the company" or "I like him/her."

Although the lack of any kind of productivity guideline is a problem—you cannot really call "Do everything you can possibly do and work as hard as you can" a guideline— it is also a boost to power building. If about half the people in an industry such as banking or accounting are not entirely certain what the bottom line is (that is, keeping the client, making the loan, or finishing the tax return), it reduces the competition for those who do understand exactly how power moves within such organizations.

It is surprising how many longtime bankers fail to see the changing power bases in banks. But let's not pick on accounting and banking. In some ways business practices in these industries are quite straightforward and sane. Contrast them with the anomalous lot of people in health care. Is a hospital really a nonprofit organization? Not always, and certainly not by choice, whatever its legal status! Unless you look carefully at an industry you cannot see its internal features or its resemblance to others you have studied.

As we look at each type of organization, within a broad category, we will look at those organized for profit first, then those organized as nonprofit. Even though there are a growing number of hospitals organized to earn profits, we will group them with the not-for-profit ones because they have the same kind of management mentality and physician problems.

ACCOUNTING: POWER BUILDING BY PERSONALITY

One of the dilemmas every new BA in Accounting faces is the question of how to become a partner in a "Big Eight" (or any other) public accounting firm. He or she has heard all of the loser legends of alumni who worked very hard and effectively for ten years only to be told, once they had reached the manager level and were eligible to be voted into partnership, that they were destined to remain career managers. This has most often been the fate of women, however competent. At this writing the number of female partners in Big Eight firms is disproportionately small. Most of those who did not make partner were outplaced to client firms. Often the clues that this was to be a manager's fate were somewhere between subtle and nonexistent. As any partner would point out, it would not be in the firm's best interests to demotivate a manager with the news of his or her ultimate disposition.

The weeding out process was swifter for people who were told at the end of three years that they would never make partner. No firm has publicly developed a truthful set of criteria for who does make partner and who does not. After all, present partners vote for new partners; that presumably accounts for the mystery in the process. If you want to play games, ask partners at any Big Eight accounting firm how they got to be partners. If you are not familiar with public accounting or its sister businesses, investment banking, consulting, and law, the only game in town is a partnership. It is not just the greater income and greater risk—though firms speak softly of these—it is the cachet which envelops people at cocktail parties who can say, "Yes,

I'm a partner with Arthur Andersen."

Since the desired end in a public accounting firm is clearly defined, and the people able to pursue it are also clearly defined (they are either consultants or CPAs), why is the path to partnership so muddied by myth and deliberate misstatement? Here is the problem: Power building in accounting firms rests on several assumptions which could not be discussed openly without casting doubt on the whole system.

Assumption One: The most technically competent people are the most valuable ones. Accounting firms act on this by making a great fuss over the college grade point averages of the young people they recruit. This is also true in management consulting, law, and most financial institutions. The most prestigious firms recruit exclusively from "name" universities. (The recruits are almost always quite young, as many returning women in their thirties and forties, with exceptionally high academic averages, learned when they tried to break into the Big Eight after they had gotten their degrees.) A B student is unlikely to be as eagerly sought after as a straight A student, particularly if the A student is presentable. If the A student is athletic, he or she is worth extra points. A C student, even one with sterling personal qualities, will usually not be hired by one of the Big Eight firms, unless she or he is the scion of a local partner or of the firm's largest and most firmly anchored client. The C student is usually not on a partnership track, and is referred to as a "charity hire." The firm hopes that this person will get some experience and move on.

Professors' recommendations are also said to count in hiring decisions. Firms are most likely to listen to unsolicited testimonials from faculty they know and respect. Grades are supposed to measure technical competence and predict an early passage of the Certified Public Accountant's examination which saves both firms and individuals time and expense.

Assumption Two: Technical excellence does not really mean much unless the person has the sort of personal and professional style that pleases not only clients but the partners who will ultimately vote on new partners. In choosing between pleasing partners and pleasing clients, most of the partners we talked with said there was no contest. They also pointed out that aspiring partners should please the present partners at all costs, or they will not have any sponsors or even one sponsor. If you are not somebody's protégé, no one looks after your best interests; no one sees to it that you get on the right audits so you can meet and impress the more powerful partners. When this occurs, you are probably destined to remain a career manager, with no hope of eventual partnership. At worst, lack of a sponsor might make you a candidate for outplacement or even slated for outright dismissal.

Partnership by personality has been changing, as long-term relationships with clients become harder to build and maintain. The problem for supervisors and managers in firms has been that pleasing the client does not guarantee pleasing the partner, especially as clients begin to change accounting firms simply for the sake of change. Several Fortune "500" corporations have publicly announced that they think changing auditors at regular intervals causes the new accounting firm to try harder. In many firms, the tendency to make the manager a scapegoat in order to protect the partner when a client leaves is very strong. Consider the alternative. Should the partner take the heat? What would this do to the hierarchy?

Since the service an accounting firm supplies—time and

advice—cannot be evaluated objectively, its employees are frequently subject to unreasonable expectations. The biggest problem is the generic nature of the service. The *Generally Accepted Accounting Principles* (GAAP) govern public accounting. One firm cannot say of another, "We're better than XYZ." All the firm has to see is its people—the more brilliant, attractive, personable, and conservative, the better. If any firm does not follow GAAP, it is probably operating illegally. Since that is extremely unlikely, the bottom line becomes some variation of relationship building and maintenance rather than working toward absolute technical perfection of the service delivered.

You, in thinking about your present career in public accounting, need to ask yourself one question: Even though I am very good technically, do I have the personal and professional style which will allow me to spend thirty to forty percent of my time selling myself to others? This is true whether you are a systems consultant, a small business specialist, or an auditor. The single exception to this division of labor is the tax specialist. Tax experts think up legal ways to reduce taxes and outwit or confound the Internal Revenue Service. As some lawyers do, tax specialists have a measurable record. How many cases were won or lost? Others in the firm recognize someone whose technical expertise in tax is visibly superior and use him/her with clients. That person will be retained and, if the tax practice is booming, will be allowed to spend less time on relationships. If the firm does not have more profitable tax business than it can handle, the pressure will be on the tax people to build relationships just as everyone else must do.

It is not only partners who have power in accounting firms. Some staff people quietly establish a lock on essential services, forcing others to reckon with them. As word processing has taken over, the word processing supervisor has become both more visible and more powerful. A partner might be able to move his or her job ahead of a manager by pulling rank but must build a political relationship with the supervisor in order to leap-frog over another partner. Partners will have long conferences about the equity of the situation, but nothing will change.

Longtime secretaries can build and hold power, especially if they are assigned to young partners or to those partners acquired through mergers or acquisitions. These secretaries train the partners in the protocol and style of partnership.

The personnel function and the personnel partner have little power. The partner in charge of each local office makes the day-to-day decisions. The partners collectively decide major issues or those that set policy. This reduces the power of any individual but vastly increases the politics and the uses of influence.

Investment banking and consulting are broadly like accounting and law in terms of power except that individual partners are even less equal. The top partners in investment banking and consulting make the decisions in a tiny tight group. The other partners exert influence. Both consulting and law firms are vulnerable to partners and also to very strong associates who can open their own shops by taking business from the parent firm or attracting clients. To keep this to a minimum, firms are always trying to keep potential competitors tied to a senior partner who shepherds them.

ACCOUNTING AND RELATED SERVICE INDUSTRIES

Profile Summary

Nature of Product/Service	Time and advice
Power Base	Personal influence and the ability to build and maintain relationships with partners and clients.
Need for Sponsor	Great, especially in auditing, management consulting, and law. More employees depart after three to ten years because of visible lack of sponsor.
Tolerance for Individual Differences	Very low. It is hard to hold on or move up in any of these fields unless you are close to the peak of the bell curve. The physically and stylistically unattractive are not likely to excel. Exception: Someone with pocket business, that is, a profitable client he or she totally controls.
Style	Sincere, all-American, regardless of racial or ethnic backround. Favors the sort of person able to fake (or have) a convincing interest in Jaycees or Lions Club, especially in smaller communities.
Future	If large companies begin to shop for brilliance and originality among consultants, bankers, lawyers, and accountants, and to change from firm to firm as they discover more in one place than another, it will force a reevaluation of how to get and hold onto business. These service businesses will always give the client whatever he or she wants once that is identified.

BANKING/FINANCIAL CONSULTING SERVICES: WHAT IS THE NEW GAME ANYWAY?

Until the early 1980s, paths to power in commercial banking and other financial institutions and in brokerage houses were clear. It was merely a question of pleasing superiors, maintaining a quiet and appropriately middle-class professional and personal lifestyle, and waiting for your superiors to move up or on. Commercial banking was thought the place to be if a person wanted money, respect, and not too much trouble or risk. Power mongers were not particularly attracted to banking—not enough risk except in real estate, oil, and mergers. These were other, higher paying ways to get into those games. In the late 1970s the ten largest banks recruited MBAs heavily from the top ten graduate business programs. It was a love match. The idea that MBAs might be imperfectly trained to deal with the 1980s never occurred to top management in these businesses.

The honeymoon is now over. Power building in banking is currently a confused and confusing process. The economy has made the old, comfortable rules obsolete. Commercial lending is not as consistently and predictably profitable as it once was—or now seems in retrospect to have been. Being well "connected," except in small towns which are correspondents of much larger banks, does not help as much as it once did. Bankers are actually expected to be both technically competent and creative! Banking, in order to survive, is going to have to recruit and reward people with ideas for profitable new financial instruments which can be mass marketed. For those who had previously looked upon banking as a lush preserve for people who could build and preserve relationships at endless lunches in the bank's executive dining room, this is quite shocking. The bottom line today is profit. Where is the profit in excellent relationships with shaky executives in unprofitable companies?

Relationships and relationship management may still provide a good living but will not meet the needs of the very ambitious. Only the continuous development and marketing of new or improved financial services can do that. Bankers are looking at cash management and product development for new and more reliable sources of revenue. The people in operations are in the ascendance because it is possible to make money in operations. It is no longer entirely a cost center. Small banks even sell the software that their systems people develop. Small internal consulting groups can take business from accounting firm management consulting groups as they solve customers' problems. In other words, power builders in banking are going to have to rethink most of their prior assumptions.

It is also important to consider the amount and kind of power available in banking versus the risks. As many manufacturing businesses became less desirable (for example, high-risk loans on aging ideas and older equipment), banks flirted with high technology start-up companies. Only someone with an engineering background and considerable electronics expertise could understand and evaluate the risk a bank assumed in lending to a start-up company. Analyzing the balance sheet, however exhaustively this was done, just did not help if the analyzer was unable to form any judgment on the potential profitability of the product. For instance, if the start-up company makes microchips, and the president of this company says his are better, as do some of the bank's people, who really knows? Are the Japanese poised to launch an even better one next week? Electronics was not the only problem area; there were also service businesses seeking start-up capital.

Enter the venture capitalists in large numbers. They siphoned off some of the bank's higher risk but also higher profit potential businesses. They built relationships not solely with money to lend but with money plus technical and managerial expertise.

This leaves banks approaching the middle 1980s searching for new sources of revenue and new ways to think about commercial lending. Not every bank has felt the change. It will take large banks a long time to respond to the need for different kinds of expertise. Many will continue to recruit MBAs with finance or marketing majors. The smarter ones will look for engineers, marketing people, and latent entrepreneurs. These people can, if banking interests them, rise rather spectacularly because they can move easily into the highest profit areas of lending. People whose chief skills are relationships and financial analysis will be the handmaidens of the new risk takers. If your technical expertise is nonexistent, your next skills should be analytical. Without either of these skills, you will not be a power builder in banking. If you became a specialist in a particular area, or if you were the protégé of someone powerful within the industry, you might be an exception.

At one time, people in personnel and human resource development had some opportunity for power building within large banks. With the lessening emphasis on affirmative action (banks are loaded with underpaid and underused women attracted by prestige and stability) and the death of quality-of-work-life movements, personnel is on the wane. As banks anxiously court high-risk/high-reward businesses, personnel will continue to decline. Who would trust personnel to distinguish the merely competent potential employee from the potential entrepreneur? Managers are going to be forced into a much riskier, more active role in the selection process, leaving personnel to complete the paper-work. At this writing banks are already beginning to replace personnel department recruiters with commercial lenders who are sent to universities to scout talent. Some are actively stealing talent from other banks.

Computer illiterates are no longer viable in any area of banking. Since they exist, however, those who are familiar with computers have an advantage in power building. The boss who cannot program in BASIC, access computer data from a terminal, or use the electronic mail machine will be at the mercy of those who can. He or she will be as vulnerable to power grabbers as non-French-speaking visitors in France are to the French.

Other financial businesses, such as stock brokerage firms, are changing internally as well. Well-connected stock-brokers used to make large commissions, and those with the highest volume of transactions were powerful within their firms. Some still are. But many firms have developed new financial instruments, such as the money market accounts, which have not necessarily helped brokers increase revenue and income. The stock market has not been consistently interesting. Talent has left many brokerage firms for start-up businesses. Those people remaining face increased competition from the discount brokerage houses, financial instruments sold through other outlets, and now from banks that offer insured money market accounts. As in manufacturing, both the unpredictability and instability of the economy have changed the internal power structure.

In the next few years the people moving up in brokerage houses will be those who invent or modify financial instruments that can be mass marketed. The idea people will move solidly into control. Again, relationships will be important but not nearly as much as in the past. How do you establish relationships with a million or ten or twenty million people? Relationships with institutional investors will also be less important because those investors ultimately seek advice wherever the best advice may be available. An aristocracy of advisers is developing within some brokerage firms independent of the research department. If the people who give the most profitable advice can also build and hold relationships, both internally and externally, they will be more powerful.

Insurance companies are facing many of the same problems of other financial institutions. Working women, a growing and largely untapped market segment, are resistant to whole life insurance; indeed, they resist any kind of life insurance other than that provided free or at low cost as a company benefit. Women can sell insurance but do so mostly to traditional men. Power levers in insurance companies will go to the innovators who figure out either new approaches to growth segments of the market or new instruments that the market will buy. At present, the salesperson with the biggest numbers still reigns. The future seems to favor not the individual high producer but the person with ideas that can be marketed to very large groups at low cost.

BANKING, FINANCIAL CONSULTING SERVICES, AND INSURANCE COMPANIES

Profile Summary

Nature of Product/Service	Money and advice on making more of it. There must be a product difference.
Power Base	Profitable ideas, technical analysis, building and holding relationships.
Need for Sponsor	It helps but is not as essential to the creative, bright person as it is in accounting. If your ideas make money, it is obvious. More important is self-

motivation. This is paramount in insurance companies and brokerage houses. Small-town banks, insurance agencies, and brokerage houses demand sponsorship because in smaller communities connections still equal money.

Tolerance for Individual Differences	Growing. As fewer baby boomers join either country clubs or the Junior League, because they are working on careers to the exclusion of traditional pastimes, methods of getting business must change. Health clubs are replacing country clubs, thereby changing who and under what circumstances people mix. Fitness is an under-fifty phenomenon. Truly quirky people, especially if they are physically unattractive, must expect closet jobs.
Style	Low-key, heavy on the facts and numbers. The jolly banker, broker, or agent is out of step with current trends. Favors those who are serious, moderately trendy, and not overly or overtly ambitious.
Future	A sober and sobering period filled with questions about which services to provide, at what cost, and to whom. A rethinking of the whole commerical lending concept, a concern for the impact of technology, and still, for many banks, the fear of interstate banking. Insurance companies and brokerage houses continue to find weaknesses in their marketing strategies. Whole life insurance is in trouble.

HEALTH CARE: WHO IS IN CHARGE?

About ten percent of the GNP is consumed by health care and nearly seven and one-half percent of the work force is part of the industry. Nowhere is it easier to see both the negative and positive qualities of the nonprofit mentality than in the health care industry; nowhere is the government's influence felt as deeply or resented more heartily. Even the nonprofit influence is not always clear or total. Hospitals are profit-generating machines overlaid with a nonprofit mentality. From a power building point of view they are many-faceted and are full of power niches. It is almost impossible to talk about hospitals without pointing out how different they are from almost every other kind of organization.

In theory, most hospitals are organized as nonprofit organizations to fulfill a "mission." Hospitals spend countless hours and large sums of money drafting mission statements detailing an idealistic philosophy of health care delivery. They do not really attempt to institute this philosophy, especially if they are located in large metropolitan areas. In reality, they want to serve those patients who can and will pay. With increasingly sophisticated accounting systems they now use industrial methods to measure productivity, allocate costs, and measure their surpluses (profits) or losses.

Hospitals are greatly influenced by—some are even run by—doctors. Even though doctors spend most of their working lives in nonprofit institutions, they do not manage their private practices on a nonprofit basis at all! They are really entrepreneurs. Their interests are mainly individual, and they are not necessarily team players.

Physicians have had in the past, and will always have, tremendous power in hospitals. They will always influence, and in some communities control, the administrators, although indirectly. Some even take management courses and become CEOs. However, the power balance in hospitals is currently changing to favor the administrators; more people are deciding for themselves which hospital to use rather than letting physicians make that choice for them. This weakens the power of the physician and strengthens the hospital's hand. A doctor's power has always rested squarely on how many hospital beds he or she could fill and keep filled with paying customers. After all, if physicians cannot control their patients, then they cannot threaten to move to another hospital.

The health care industry has a major style problem that anyone who is interested in this particular arena must understand. While it is perfectly possible for IBM executives to say, "I hope we put AT&T out of business," and for AT&T people to say, "I'd love to see IBM go under," it is not possible for people at one hospital to say, "I'd like to see Divine Sufferer Hospital go out of business. If we can help them do so, we will." In other words, hospitals and the entire health care delivery system are burdened with and stagger under a facade of public good. It simply is not possible to speak openly of one's interests or intentions. The resulting hypocrisy has a negative effect on the organization's style and forces everyone to package every statement, confusing everybody involved. Unless you can adjust your style to say one thing consistently and mean another, you will have a problem because, for power builders in this sector, the only power style is one that does not acknowledge the highly competitive nature of health care. You have to adopt the philosophy of someone who would wreck a competitor's research to ensure receiving the Nobel prize, someone who would also speak very highly of his or her victim on all public occasions. Those who refuse to play the game will not build power. The administrator who says publicly, "This hospital is a business, and I'm running it with sound business principles," will not prosper. It is important to understand the pivotal role of doctors in the power structure and why their values are different from the other players in the organization.

Recently we did some focus group research with doctors. (Focus groups are a way of getting people to talk about their feelings and attitudes toward issues, institutions, and people.) The results will interest those who long to ascend the hospital power ladder either administratively or medically. These groups were designed to explore physicians' attitudes toward hospitals, fellow professionals, patients, and each other. As you look at the results, ask yourself what the implications are for power building in hospitals or clinics.

The strongest finding from our focus groups was that most physicians see hospitals as the people equivalent to the Sears auto bay. They would like to roll their patient in, repair or replace defective parts, and roll him or her out again without ever having to develop any social, professional, or emotional attachments to the hospital or to any of its administrators. Nurses are the exception because many doctors do not perceive them as part of the hospital hierarchy; they view the nurses as their own personal possessions! Nurses stand with doctors in every sense of the word, according to the doctors.

Physicians, as most will admit, are always on the verge of burnout. Many of the behavior mannerisms they display in hospitals serve as defense mechanisms against any or further involvement with co-workers. They are patient-centered and staff wary. This fact bears repeating. They are focused on the patient and anxious to avoid involvements with the staff, especially the administrative staff, which they see as the source of problems, restrictions, politics, and impertinence.

Physicians generally do not want any directive or policy-making power within the hospital. This kind of power is time consuming and emotionally involving with a minimum payoff. What they really want is negative power (that is, veto power). A physician does not care if the hospital wants to put a pasta bar in the cafeteria unless it affects his or her interests. As one doctor said, "I don't care what they do in this hospital as long as they don't do anything I don't agree with." "They" is always the administration.

Physicians are groupies. They do not act alone. If one physician is angry about a policy, he or she will not discuss it with a hospital CEO—unless it is just a tantrum and not serious—until he has lined up physician support for his position and scouted possible opponents. That is why every physician is annually a member of at least one or two free-floating opposition groups. These groups tend to be specifically issue-oriented, and the physicians' behavior follows from the desire for veto power.

As a result of their training and temperament, physicians dislike generalizing and are reluctant to trust. They do not want to build trust relationships except with nurses whom they feel they can control. Most physicians also believe that nurses are sympathetic to them.

Every physician has known the terror of an occasional misdiagnosis. While this is an unavoidable hazard in medicine, it is an intolerable hazard in human relations. Therefore, if you convince a doctor that a hospital policy is reasonable, you have only convinced him on the basis of one incident or set of facts. Only that one policy is reasonable. The rest have not been evaluated yet. Each "case" must be diagnosed individually. This makes it difficult for nonphysician power builders to move from building relationships with physicians to maintenance. They are caught in a time warp, forever in the building stage.

Teaching physicians to trust nonphysicians and to recognize a commonality of interests is very difficult. They do
not see the advantages, and they do not like to share. A
referral to another physician is not sharing. It is professional
tit for tat. Many physicians feel they do not need political
relationships. When push comes to shove, they push rather
than negotiate. Younger ones, seeing the surplus of physicians in some parts of the country, tend to be more flexible.
However, the process of educating successful physicians in
their own self-interests so that they will trust and share rather
than push is long and complicated, and entails frequent
repetition. Politically, physicians are slow learners.

It is better financially if a doctor's practice takes the
traditional, negative-interference-only attitude. Doctors who
think and care about nonmedical problems create a problem
for other physicians and also for hospital administrators.
That is why so many hospitals have problems acculturating
their younger physicians. It is also why they prefer that
younger ones be in group practices with older doctors who
will provide the appropriate role models.

Doctors are always outsiders. It is partly the nature of
medicine and partly the kind of person that the medical
profession attracts. This makes them very vulnerable to
people who share insider gossip. Physicians have insatiable
appetites for insider power gossip and less interest in people
gossip. They are observers. Still, they want to feel some
minimal connection, and gossip is the vehicle for this. Only
doctors nearing senility and/or retirement care about sex
stories, particularly intrastaff sex stories.

Administrators drive doctors wild by not fighting every
battle with equal vigor. As physicians see it, an administrator
who gives in is not compromising. He or she is weak. Weak
people are not predictable, and predictability is one of the

qualities physicians revere the most. For example, the physicians lobby for an operating room policy change. They meet with everyone in the hospital who has influence. In three months, over the administrator's still-warm body, a part of the policy change is made. Great relief and cheering emanate from the doctors' lounge. A month later, without identifiable provocation, the rest of the policy change is put into place. The physicians are aghast. How did it happen? Why weren't they consulted in advance? It is ultimately what they wanted, but they are insulted that they were not consulted.

For the health care power builder, it is apparent that learning to work with and through physicians in power building is vital. It is not possible to be powerful in any organization with physicians unless you can build and maintain warm, strong relationships with them. This takes time and requires meeting an unmet need. For most physicians that need is political updating. They want to know who is important and who is not. They respect people who get to the point instantly and do not ask them what they think. (You can usually infer the answer if you really want to know.)

The religious overtones or affiliations, however tenuous, of many health care providers are often ignored by power builders because so few members of the founding religious group are even visible, much less still in management. This is a serious mistake. The hospital's religious affiliation provides clues as to what kind of packaging sells. To ignore it is to misread important signals and lose opportunities to influence others. For example, do not announce that your wife is having her tubes tied if you work for Divine Sufferer Hospital. The only thing worse would be if you are female and ask if the abortion can be done there!

HEALTH CARE INDUSTRY

Profile Summary

Nature of Product/Service	Health care and medical advice.
Power Base	If there are MDs, it is influence with them. If doctors play a minor role, it is medical administrators.
Need for Sponsor	Not great if one is particularly skilled at politics. The nature of the hierarchy is such that doctors usually only sponsor doctors and the administrators' sponsorship is sub rosa.
Tolerance for Individual Differences	Medium to high within role and philosophical limits. A woman doctor or administrator can wear bulletproof polyester so long as she packages her message in the language of the hospital's mission statement. The same is true in clinics, HMOs, nursing homes, etcetera.
Style	You must evince absolute bone-deep sincerity when discussing the moral rectitude of medical personnel. A respectful "you-know-best" attitude toward physicians is essential for power building. An analytical style helps move the group decision-making process along, as does a relentlessness in sticking to the point.
Future	The government continues to bedevil health care. This gives the establishment the glooms. Other than that, the whole industry is booming and will continue to do so, side-stepping here and hopping there. Most Americans still want state-of-the-art health care.

NONPROFIT ORGANIZATIONS: THE VALUE OF LONGEVITY

Power building in nonprofit organizations is always interesting because both the style and the values are so different from those in business. About twenty-three percent of all workers are employed by nonprofit organizations, and if you want to do a job which exists only in the nonprofit sector, you must learn how to become a part of the power system.

Nonprofit organizations fall into two groups: (1) public sector organizations, that is, all branches of government and quasi-governmental agencies, and (2) the private nonprofit organizations, such as health and welfare agencies, associations, and societies, and other enterprises legally organized as not-for-profit. The nonprofits wanted steady, committed, and not necessarily ambitious employees who would stay a long time. Until very recently the goals of people working for nonprofits and the responses of nonprofits were clear. The people who chose nonprofits wanted job security and were willing to take a smaller salary in exchange for this security. Some wanted to feel that they were "helping." Sadly, many thought that they were avoiding the competitiveness and politics of business. In reality, nonprofits provide more of both.

If anything, nonprofits have suffered more from inflation and recession than have companies, with the exception of hospitals. Their leadership was often timid. Resources were almost always smaller than in companies. The brightest, most ambitious people who had wandered into the nonprofit sector—often by mistake—easily moved into the profit sector once they realized the inherent financial instability of the agency or group they worked for. The people left behind were not risk takers, not action-oriented, and not power builders in the larger sense, although one individual agency head might be in the throes of megalomania.

If you look at the huge number of people who work in this sector, it is easy to visualize them as a faceless mass. They are not. In many ways there are as many subgroups and special interest groups as there are in any industry. For instance, there are some entrepreneurial and risk-taking people working for branches of government, in health care, and in social service agencies. The majority are security-oriented, although there is still a vocal minority that is not.

Traditionally, power building in nonprofits has rested on two points: longevity and personal relationships. However, as nonprofits experienced greater financial difficulties in the late 1970s and early 1980s, the balance of power has shifted to fund raisers and marketers. Even the governmental agencies are feeling the need for better public relations with those who fund them.

There is a time lag in nonprofits that creates followers rather than leaders. This is a result of the low level of risk taking that most of these organizations attempt. For example, just as most corporations had exhausted the possibilities of Management by Objectives (MBO) and had begun to emphasize different strategies, many nonprofits, figuring MBO was now sufficiently debugged, began to take it up. Imagine the dismay of the people who had left industry for the less stressful environments of nonprofits only to find themselves going through the same hideous MBOs again.

Relationships in nonprofit organizations are built on more ideological grounds than in the profit sector. For instance, it really matters in a social service agency who likes poor people and who finds them merely tolerable. The reason it matters is that, like hospitals, most nonprofits have an ideological cast. The social service agencies tend to be the last refuge of the 1960s person who wants to "help." These aging hippies tend to be over forty and are caught in an ideological time warp. Since by now most are in management positions, it can be fatal to power building to indicate, however subtly, that you think of these people and their views as dinosaurs. If you cannot work with and for them, then you cannot work in many nonprofits. Always test to see the style of the person to whom you will be reporting.

Ideology has another important impact in nonprofits. It defines the limits of permissible relationships. While it is perfectly possible for IBM and Xerox people to mix socially, many social service agency administrators are anxious when their people mix with "competitive" agencies. They do not want the hard, effective workers they have to mix with anybody who might tell them about better job opportunities, especially if they have just agreed to a salary freeze.

Protocol is usually tighter and more strictly observed in nonprofits because, lacking the financial perks of profit-making organizations, this may be a manager's main high. For instance, in Roman Catholic universities non-Catholics and lay Catholics are expected to address priests working in nonpriestly roles as "Father," though this is purely a title. It is also one of the chief perks of a Catholic priest toiling in the philosophy department as the department's enrollment evaporates. Attendance at quasi-social functions is very much a part of relationship building. If you exclude yourself from the duller after-work festivities, you are marking yourself as an outsider.

No discussion of nonprofits would be complete without an examination of the role of longevity in power building. It is not possible for a secretary with two years' experience to challenge a secretary with twenty years' experience, no matter what the facts may be in a particular case. In nonprofit organizations longevity demands respect. There usually is no formal seniority system as a union would organize it. There is, however, a reverence for seniority that would warm a union organizer's heart. The theory once again is that respect is not earned, it accrues over time.

The nonprofit organizations which have kept people past all usefulness are legendary. They are of interest here only because they illustrate a mentality which must be taken into account in power building. For example, secretaries to department heads and administrators frequently last through several regimes. They train their bosses and subtly shape the power structure. It would be difficult for a new administrator to transfer, much less fire, a long-term secretary. She has a lock on that job. This may be foreign to those who have worked in private industry, but it is true.

High-minded brutality, or brutality in the pursuit of a good cause, is condoned. If we must drive someone out before she or he is vested in the pension plan, that is okay; it leaves more for those who are already vested. It also keeps down the number of people who will be vested. Torturing someone out is the preferred style because it makes the other employees feel that the victim must have done something terrible or that he or she is leaving voluntarily!

NONPROFIT ORGANIZATIONS

Profile Summary

Nature of Product/Service	Advice or service for people unable to provide those things for themselves.
Power Base	Longevity, widespread ties within organization, ability to do favors for others, some outside (public) recognition.
Need for Sponsor	A sponsor may be the only way to learn how the system works in a nonprofit organization, especially a university or association. It is usually so necessary to clothe ideas in a particular ideology that it is difficult for those practiced in the technique to separate what they are doing from the facts.
Tolerance for Individual Differences	One of the strengths of the nonprofit environment is that it tolerates almost any eccentricity. It is a haven for all kinds of counterculture ideas and will allow people to take something to its logical extreme—say breast feeding in the classroom.
Style	The social worker's style is supreme here. Nothing is more important than measurable, palpable sincerity. If you cannot feel a gut-level interest in the population served on the task to be performed, you will not be a power builder in nonprofits. Longtime employees have disproportionate power and use it.
Future	Unless there is a resurgence of the sixties' mentality—so far not a sign of which has turned up among current college students—nonprofits outside the health care industry are going to be in for hard times. The idea of self-sacrifice does not have the appeal that it once had.

MANUFACTURING: THE AGING GIANT

American manufacturers employ only about twenty-two and one-half percent of the work force. Two-thirds of all workers are in knowledge and service industries. Since 1970, companies feeling the competition from Japan and Germany, not just in automobiles, steel, and computers but in many technical areas, have responded in interesting ways. After asking the government for greater tariff protection, they began to look at all kinds of "new" productivity schemes. This has had mixed results. From the perspective of power building, it is a profound change.

Human resource people, as opposed to time/motion engineers and labor relations consultants, are likely to become more powerful within large manufacturing firms (just as they lose influence in the service sector) as it becomes clear to top management that productivity problems cannot be cured by more money, robotics, or any single approach. Any time an organization needs a top-to-bottom rethinking of its business approach, the power structure becomes very fluid. This is especially true when top management cannot agree on, or hesitates to commit to, a single approach. To understand how different things are for manufacturers in the 1980s, consider this: The companies now being vilified for closing factories are the same ones that were so eagerly welcomed by community boosters several decades ago.

Many bright young people are eagerly looking for start-up companies to work for rather than seeking careers with such giants as the automobile manufacturers, IBM, Xerox, and aerospace companies. Part of this reflects a feeling that bigness may mean intellectual and technical sludge rather than opportunity. In response, many of the giants who were anxious to attract a more creative engineer (instead of someone who was anxious to play it safe), find a comfortable niche, and redo the same product until retirement are now courting mavericks.

Power within many manufacturing companies is flowing to the innovator, the cost cutter, and the cash manager. Having identified weaknesses in products as well as within the organization's management structure, companies are not likely to forget the recent recession. Recession mentality will linger as managers continue to reassess their positions and make changes in every area of the operation. This provides the greatest opportunity since the Great Depression for the nonconformist, the entrepreneur, and the non-MBA.

Strategic planning, as opposed to operational planning, will be a power center for the rest of the 1980s. In fact, crystal ball gazers with good track records are already in great demand. The fluidity and unpredictability of consumer demand means that marketing, while never to be neglected, is less important than planning. The question is not "How can we sell the consumer our goods?" but "What will the consumer buy and what does the consumer want?" If you think of operational planning as the process of charting a path from point A to point B, you can visualize strategic planning as defining both point A and point B. It is a process of initiating and deciding on a path of action rather than responding to decisions made elsewhere.

Another power point in industry will be the creative use of increased technology. Even if robotics become commonplace in the 1980s, figuring out new and more cost-effective ways to use them will increase the thinker's power. Furthermore, training present workers in high-technology skills will be important. Does that mean that the training function will increase in importance? Only if the results of training can be clearly demonstrated.

In the newest high-technology companies which provide both products and services, power will flow to those who are or seem to be ahead of the pack. This is truer than in the past because so much media attention is focused on new developments. It is now possible to pick up a business magazine and see an in-depth analysis of the technical prowess of every kind of personal computer system. The same article may predict whose software or hardware will be the best or the newest while it is still being developed. The public exposure of high-technology companies scrambles traditional internal power structures. For instance, an engineer who makes a breakthrough may be boosted into management even though he or she is still quite young and has no idea of how to manage. The line between doers and managers is blurred. This will sometimes give the traditional middle manager a power boost. He or she may be the only one who knows, even in theory, what managers are supposed to do. Knowing the role can be very handy.

Service is very important as more companies go into high-technology consumer goods. When IBM made only mainframe computers, its need to explain in the simplest terms about how such machines worked was minimal compared to its need to explain how the IBM personal computer worked. Training materials will be part of the marketing function; the product cannot be sold to a mass market without them. This means that people who can explain to the masses how to do or use something will have a ready market in the 1980s. Word processing is another power point.

Power building in high-technology industries is very time-consuming because the level of uncertainty is much higher.

Companies worry about whether the Japanese will make a new microchip obsolete before it even gets on the market. What will they do if that happens? This is not the arena for people without strong risk-taking skills. In such businesses, security-oriented souls will be on the verge of mental breakdowns.

MANUFACTURING

Profile Summary

Nature of Product/Service	All kinds of products.
Power base	Quality and quantity of ideas in three areas: product development, marketing, and productivity.
Need for Sponsor	Very important in traditional, long-established companies. The larger the overall organization, the greater the need.
Tolerance for Individual Differences	Much greater than in the past. Especially on the rise are people who can work as innovators within the system and not lose either creativity or entrepreneurial zeal.
Style	Sincerity is not necessary as long as the product sells. No-nonsense, autocratic style currently under attack by advocates of consensus-style management.
Future	A risk taker's paradise of high stakes and huge rewards.

THE GLAMOUR INDUSTRIES

The glamour industries, while employing only about five percent of the adult work force, are similar to the service businesses in terms of power building, with the exception of power resting on the creation of an illusion rather than on personality as such. If you look at the people on television, in the theater, movies, advertising, publishing, newspapers, and on radio, you will see that more than any other workers these people are literally selling their own, self-created images. They may have to please bosses, top management, or organizational types, but ultimately the public either buys or does not buy whatever they are selling. The model Cheryl Tiegs is an example. Her image seems to sell products. When it ceases to sell products, she will be out of the public eye.

Logic, predictability, and market research are frequently subordinated to instinct or what someone may call a hunch or gut feeling: "It just feels right" or "I've got a feeling for this." Everyone sells everyone else at all times. The test of greatness is not job performance but skill at selling anything and everything.

The whole idea of conventional morality is suspended in many of the glamour businesses. For instance, an advertising agency may design extremely effective ads for a particular product. The people who created the advertisements may know that the product is inferior to a nonadvertised one. People who have a value system that compels them to seek the one best product or service will find the daily and hourly compromises which are made in these businesses difficult to reconcile.

To this homely truth add the following: Most of the people in the glamour industries are there because of the thrall of glamour and excitement; they are not there because they made a conscious choice. It is rarely the sort of thing their families wanted them to do unless other family members had been successful in that field. They are there because they cannot help themselves. They have very strong needs for glamour and fame and mostly do not pretend otherwise. Ask an actor, writer, or advertising copywriter or newspaper reporter, "Why did you choose this business?" He or she is very likely to say, "This is the only thing I have ever wanted to do." That does not mean the person has never done any other kind of work, only that there is a strong drive propelling him or her toward one kind of career and one kind of reward.

All of the glamour businesses are a sudden-death playoff. People are only as good as their last review, performance, marketing meeting, story, et cetera. Therefore, power within these organizations rests entirely on influence. No one person can promise a boss or an organization that the public, or some particular segment of it, will love them as much today as yesterday or as much tomorrow as today. The glamour businesses are the highest personal and professional risks of all. They also can provide tremendous power if one is at the top in any of them.

The editor in chief of a newspaper or magazine or the editor within a publishing house who "makes" best sellers will be greatly sought after. People who need them will hang on their every word. However, a mistake will be far more costly in ego loss and dollars than in an ordinary service business. Firings are quicker and bloodier. Failing to read the public mind is considered to be just short of a criminal offense.

Since close working relationships do not have the same value that they have in other businesses, and since any kind of behavior can be tolerated, the politics will be very different from other service businesses. People will cultivate those with the ultimate decision-making power, that is, the money people, but will be less concerned with a boss, peer, or subordinate's needs or interests. Job tenure is rarely an issue. A person in the media or advertising who has never been fired from a job is thought to be mundane. Creative people have regular clashes with others who do not accept their ideas. Routiners are not the stuff of the Big Idea or the Big Sale.

People who are not highly visible in glamour businesses build power by influencing the visible people. The advertising copywriter who writes a commercial that raises the sales curve may be very much influenced by the researcher. That person tells the writer what is going on outside the narrow world of advertising. A person can choose to be influential and then surround him/herself with the people he or she thinks will ultimately be important. Most influential people have not done that; they operate on pure instinct. In no other industry does gut feeling constitute at once an excuse and a reason for everything!

One of the dangers of power within glamour industries is that since it is personalized, most of the people who succeed are recognizable public figures. Many of them find this kind of attention difficult to adjust to because they tend to crave privacy. They find privacy by insulating themselves from the public. Losing touch with the way masses of people are changing brings about the inability to predict what those same people will want to read, see, or buy. It is professional suicide but a slow death. How many of the people whose television or radio shows were cancelled or whose big advertising campaigns bombed lost touch with the subtle ways in which masses of Americans were changing? In these businesses nemesis inevitably follows hubris.

GLAMOUR INDUSTRIES

Profile Summary

Nature of Product/Service	Entertainment, information, illusion, mass marketing.
Power Base	The idea for a product, service or amusement is supreme. Profitability is everything. The ability to take both personal and professional risks is essential. Timid people cannot be powerful unless they mask this quality very cleverly.
Need for Sponsor	Since this is a personal business in the most precise meaning of the word, a sponsor is helpful but not essential. Most people rely on self-promotion, an art in itself and not to be despised. More than sponsors, access to powerful people is important. If a sponsor can help, he or she is useful.
Tolerance for Individual Differences	Highest of any kind of business. There is nothing which cannot and will not be tolerated if the profit, both actual and potential, is great enough. Most clients are extremely difficult to please, and that too will be tolerated.
Style	No pretense of sincerity is necessary so long as the individual promotes him/herself and his/her talent. An outgoing style is the dominant one. Negotiating styles do well. Political skills tend to be elementary: whom to please, whom to avoid. Personal loyalty is not as important as in other businesses. Hypocrisy is not necessary. Everyone knows that box office results are the whole show.
Future	These businesses will always be important. Anyone who thinks advertising, book

publishing, movies and television, in some form, will not be around in the long run really does not understand how essential these businesses are.

9. POWER PROBLEMS: SEX AND LIFESTYLE

OCCASIONALLY an otherwise sensible person falls in love or becomes infatuated with a co-worker. This co-worker may be a boss, a peer, or even a subordinate. Although we have already established that the only office secrets are those you have not yet heard, people persist in the belief that they can keep interested co-workers in the dark or, once discovered, keep them from turning that information into a weapon. It cannot be done. Sexual involvement undermines power and changes working relationships in many ways. One of the ironies of power is that appearances have the same effect as reality. If two people appear to be sexually involved, the effect on the power of both will be the same as if they were. Here are some of the problems close liaisons create.

1. If people talk about you personally, they will ignore or dismiss your work accomplishments in favor of your sex life, which seems to be a more exciting topic. No one can

dominate the grapevine. There is room for only a certain amount of news, both personal and professional, about any one person. The personal will overpower the professional every time. It will obscure your accomplishments and praise from the boss as people report when the two of you were last seen at the water cooler.

2. Sexual involvement causes people to selectively edit the news. If Mary Anne networks regularly with Bill, Sally, and Joan and is emotionally (and/or intimately) involved with Roger, the group's first desire will be to protect Mary Anne from bad news about Roger. They like Mary Anne. She is an important part of the group. The group may feel that they should pretend they do not know what is going on. In most cases this means no news at all. This is the last thing Mary Anne should want. She needs to know what is being said. She is taking a sizable career risk with her emotional involvement, and only the grapevine can tell her exactly how big the risk is. The same is true for Roger. If Mary Anne has any political problems, Roger will hear of them last. Neither can warn or help the other. In addition to the political risks, isolation frequently undermines the relationship itself by making them less helpful to, and less trusting of, each other.

3. If two people are involved and one is more powerful than the other, through either formal position or influence, the more powerful one is thought to protect the less powerful one. This is a consistent corporate stereotype. For example, when David becomes involved with his secretary, Marsha, it changes her relationships with all of the other secretaries by altering their perceptions of her. Marsha is doing the same work, saying the same things, and being the same person she has always been, but people are now more careful around her. She seems temporarily more powerful because

of her relationship. Even if she does not exploit the possibilities for greater power that David's interest gives her, others will interpret whatever she does as an attempt to do that. Her most casual comment on office events will be interpreted as his opinion or position. She will cease to have an individual identity or any independent position. She cannot say, "Nothing has changed," because perceptions have changed, and those are very real.

David's subordinates, other than Marsha, will also treat her differently. They will be more respectful, especially the men. They will tell themselves there is no reason to get on David's bad side by causing Marsha a problem. They will also resent having to do it.

4. Sexual relationships between peers invite comment. People feel they should take a stand. Are Doris and Bill really right for each other? Will it last? It is unusual for co-workers to organize a quarter pool betting on the outcome of the affair, but it is not unknown! During a reorganization or merger, sexual liaisons assume a tremendous importance. As people scramble for new alliances or as old ones disintegrate, two people united by other than a healthy interest in political survival become a bump in the road. They cause others to think and plan—not with them but around them. After all, if one person's interests are threatened, how will the partner respond? There is always the danger of retaliation from two people if one's partner's career is in danger. Finally, if the affair is that hot, they both may fail to concentrate on the crisis at hand. That makes them, at best, unreliable.

By far the greatest risk of an office affair and the best reason to look for liaisons outside the office is this: Sex gives enemies a weapon that can be used at any time, even years after the affair ends. If one of the two people is married, sex is the ideal weapon. Those using it can rest piously on the side of conventional morality.

Consider the case of a bank CEO. Allen has been having an affair with Virginia (a marketing manager in the bank) for twenty years. He and she have been seen openly at company functions, at conventions, and on other official occasions. Whatever the relationship of Allen and his wife, apparently it is one of mutual tolerance. No one has ever heard the word divorce mentioned. Allen appears with his wife Jane at the annual employee Christmas party. Jane and Virginia are very cordial.

One day the bank's senior management and three of the board of directors decide that Allen should retire. He resists, arguing strongly for retention based on his performance and the bank's excellent profits during his tenure. They threaten to expose his relationship with Virginia. They point out how public exposure would weaken the bank's credibility in the community. (No one ever questions this sort of statement even though, in fact, the sexual habits of a bank CEO are rarely as important as his fiscal habits.) If he forces the board to expose his relationship, it will influence his financial settlement from the bank. He finally agrees to go. Two weeks after his departure, Virginia is forced to resign. She goes to a competitive bank.

How is it possible that sex could be so effective a weapon when the relationship has been going for twenty years? Surely the shock value, if any, has worn off by now. What is going on here really has nothing to do with the moral problems of extramarital sex. Allen is vulnerable because, while the informal system is fully appraised of his relationship with Virginia, the formal system is, and must remain, officially ignorant. By creating an open break between systems he hands his enemies a weapon. Had his affair been "secret," the fire power would have been greater. He would have risked both public and intracompany exposure.

A second example of the weapon power of sex would be the marketing manager who has had an affair with a subordinate. He and she lived together for several months. In heated moments he made some rash promises of all he would do for her professionally, notably help her get promoted within the department. They broke up, and she sued him and the company for sexual harassment. Although she had a ridiculously weak case, his power base is destroyed. Even if she drops the suit and leaves quietly, he will have great difficulty recovering power. He appears terminally weak because he allowed himself to be put in such a ridiculous position. Top management will say he should have anticipated it. Many top management people believe that men are unduly influenced by sex and must guard against such weakness. It is interesting that, outside literature, women are never thought to be influenced by passion. Women who give up their careers for men are out of fashion.

In fact, men aren't the only ones who find sex a problem in power building. A woman has several areas of vulnerability, which surface when she gets involved with a male co-worker.

1. Women still come up against top management's tacit endorsement of the double standard. The more conservative the organization, the more this is holy writ. Even if top management seems enlightened, it is a pretty sure bet they unofficially believe that "boys will be boys, but the girls should say no!"

Suppose Bill and Liz, two data processing consultants, are both assigned to spend ten weeks on an important client's computer installation in Des Moines. They are both single. They meet at the airport in Denver on Sunday nights and take the same plane back to Denver on Friday nights. They are both putting in ten-hour days. The installation is not in downtown Des Moines; it is in an industrial park on the outskirts. The motel their practical boss selected is half a mile down the road from the work site. They share a rental car.

After a week of joint dinners, followed by dinner for one, Bill suggests that they will both have terminal cabin fever before the installation is completed. They begin to spend evenings going to the movies, to a local shopping center, driving around town, and sitting and talking. Bill and Liz turn out to have quite a lot in common. They like each other.

At this point nobody at the home office cares because Bill and Liz are not in the office grapevine. Other than an occasional call on the boss's part, checking to see whether they are getting the job done, they are off in a void. By now they are enjoying each other's company a great deal. They are thinking of themselves as a team. Enter the effects of chemistry. If there is any chemistry between these two people, there is going to be trouble. It will not be personal trouble; they may get married and live happily ever after together. The trouble will be political when both return to the home office. They are not going to be able to convince even a semicomatose colleague that the he and she who left on assignment did not return as a couple.

For him it may be a minor problem, if the boss thinks highly of him. For her it is a major and a twofold problem as well. She has bucked the double standard publicly. A motel in Des Moines is public no matter what actually happened. She has also established a relationship that does not allow her boss to fantasize himself into the picture, however much he might deny any such intention. Her career will almost inevitably be undermined.

2. A woman risks the retaliation of other women in the office based on their perception that she is using unfair tactics. This is a major change in women's values. Sleeping your way to the top or even just having fun was not a power reducer until the competition among women, in supervisory and middle management positions, sharpened considerably in the late seventies. As companies make "corrections" in the promotions given women in the seventies, any deviation from the "rules" will elicit retaliation. The rules include a prohibition against mixing sex and business. Women still believe in group guilt. If one woman gets involved with a co-worker, it threatens all of the women in the company. Women believe that top management will deny all women advancement because one of them got out of line.

The nature of competition among women is an almost insuperable obstacle to their firmly bonding together in organizations. Most women are trained from childhood to compete with each other at the most personal level possible. They do not compete as athletes, dancers, or cheerleaders, but personally, on their physical makeup and personality. There was only one football captain, one basketball captain, one prom queen. There could be only one winner but many losers.

The minute a sexual relationship (or one that appears to be sexual) comes to light, women cross off the male half of the duo. He has been won. He is out of the running. Many women feel diminished or defeated, even though it was a contest in which they were not even possible entrants. After all, the campaign was being staged in Des Moines while the rest of the potential competitors were in Denver.

Practically, it makes no difference. If any of the women who work with or for the data processing consultant feel that Liz's relationship with her colleague moves her ahead, however slightly, they will use a scalpel on her reputation in the grapevine. This is still true in 1984, even though most women know the double standard is unfair to all women and that women should support other women for the greater good of the group.

You might think that women respond jealously to other women in such situations. Looked at carefully, it is usually a power problem, not relationship envy. Women want power at least as much as men do. Never assume otherwise.

Although admittedly an extreme example, the following story is not really far outside the mainstream. All of the professional-level women in a research laboratory organized a women's network which would meet regularly during the lunch hour to talk about work-related issues. When it became known that one of the members had had an affair with her boss and coincidentally had gotten a promotion in grade level, the other thirty-two women in the network asked her not to join them again. When she protested that she had earned the promotion and that the two events were not connected, she was told by one of the leaders that she had been "insensitive to other women's concerns and had hurt their interests by giving management something to snicker about."

LIFESTYLE PROBLEMS

If you had to choose whether an office affair or an odd lifestyle was more disastrous to power building, it would be a toss-up. There are certain lifestyles that seem to be every bit as harmful to power building as any kind of sexual liaison. Here are the problem lifestyles.

1. Any lifestyle which obviously separates you from most of the other workers reduces power. For instance, if you not only do not drink liquor but you will not enter any place in which liquor is served, you will have a lifestyle problem in a company where booze lubricates business relations. Be advised that members of Alcoholics Anonymous and even some active members of the Mormon Church go into bars. They never drink spirits, but they are there for the same business purposes as those who do drink. Another example would be someone who tries to order unprocessed food in a French restaurant and decries the added ingredients in entrées. This is not only bad manners, it is a power problem as well. The problem is isolation from the mainstream. The isolation defeats any attempt to build an alliance. Instead it presents a you-against-them image.

2. Any lifestyle which keeps you from participating in the activities that others in your department or division engage in will reduce your power. If you can never play softball after work because you are engaged in rock farming, it is going to be a problem. If you can never attend an evening meeting because you would not dream of letting a sitter put the kids to bed, you are not going to be a power builder. It is not your agenda but your inflexibility that will keep others from getting to know you well enough to build relationships with you. This can even affect your ability to get the job done, if you must collaborate with others on projects. Without a cultivated sense of comradeship it is difficult to get extra effort from others when you need it.

3. A lifestyle so much more affluent than your peers that they will not entertain you in their homes, even after you have asked them to yours, can be detrimental to power

building. If you are obviously much better off financially than your peers, your boss may be impressed. However, you are going to have to tone down your style enormously if you are going to build power with your peers. If you win hands down in the lifestyle game, where is the equality of the office competition? If you press your advantage, your peers may even sabotage you. It may not be fair, but it happens everywhere.

For example, a staff accountant comes from an affluent family. Instead of the scruffy apartment, which is common to twenty-three-year-olds, decorated in old travel posters and shared with at least one other person, he has a nicely decorated one-bedroom apartment all to himself in the city's high-rent district. He does not, as his contemporaries do, give bring-your-own-booze parties. He serves brand name liquor and imported beer. He ought to be saving it for his family and nonwork associates. Inevitably it is going to harm his relationships with his peers. They will hesitate to include him, even in afterwork socializing at the local watering hole.

4. You are troubled by indecision. You hate to commit to anything with even a whiff of permanence. You would hate to sign a two-year lease, even if you saved money, since you do not know if you will want to live where you are next year, much less a year after that. This lack of decisiveness causes others to question not whether you will fulfill your commitments—you would do that—but whether you will be on the job for more than a few months. As one man said, "I like to stay packed, just in case." That kind of attitude will cause others to exclude you from quasi-business occasions. If you care about power building, you will have to develop a greater sense of commitment. Otherwise, the desire to hang loose is going to undermine all of

your efforts to become more powerful. It will also cause both your peers and your superiors to take you less seriously.

5. You are really not interested in work. Your mind is on other things. You do your job, but the passion of your life is not achievement. You would like a good job so long as it does not interfere with life. This attitude causes others to see you essentially as a drop-in. You are not part of the mainstream. In fact, in the eighties, anyone who is not very serious about work will find power building difficult. People can tell from your conversation that you are oriented away from, not toward, work. They will hesitate to form alliances with you because they think any problems will cause you to withdraw or lower, rather than raise, your level of effort.

NONPROBLEMS

Surprisingly, being gay is not a lifestyle problem in most companies so long as you do not violate the same sexual taboos heterosexuals have to observe. Being handicapped does not keep you from being powerful once people overcome their tendency to be initially awkward in the presence of a physically handicapped person. Intense religiosity won't hurt as long as you don't seek converts. Politics is rarely taken seriously unless your personal politics are radically different from the company's official or unofficial position.

It is always better to mute your differences from the mainstream if you are building power. Not only does that make it easier for others to work with you, it separates your work and personal lives. That separation will help you keep both your sanity and your perspective during the unsettled times ahead. Consider your work a role to be well played and concentrate on doing just that.

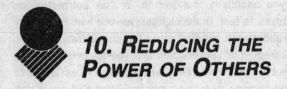

10. REDUCING THE POWER OF OTHERS

MEL Peppler's fellow CPA in the tax department, Gary, took a continuing education course in acting. Suddenly he was Clint Eastwood, Cary Grant, and Gregory Peck all wrapped into one. Gary began to use his newfound charm on their mutual boss. The boss began to make unfavorable comparisons between Mel, whom he now found rather shy and unpolished, and the blooming Gary. With promotion time three months away it was important to get the boss's mind back on productivity, where Mel would have the advantage. But how?

Occasionally, even the most benevolent, team-spirited soul realizes there is no way to reach his/her goals or even get the job done without doing surgery on someone else's power base. You want to stop someone from doing something and, by reducing his or her power, keep the person from causing the same problem again. In this chapter we will look at a step by step process for analyzing where a

competitor's power base is vulnerable (blind spot) and how
to use that information to reduce the person's power.

DIAGNOSIS: SURGERY

Do not assume that because we are working on someone
else's base it is necessarily an attempt at backstabbing. Surgery may be needed to help the organization reach a positive
goal or protect its flanks. For example, an employee is
blocking your effort to finish a particular job. Direct confrontation has failed. Unless something is done, the entire
department may be unable to function. Unless you combat
this and undercut the obstructor, you are not doing your
job.

To illustrate: Several years ago two professors were involved in a major power struggle that threatened the survival
of an already weakened School of Education at a major
university. The dean refused to interfere, reasoning that it
would widen faculty involvement if he took official notice.
The faculty members continued to squabble just as the ac-
creditation committee was about to arrive and the university
was about to make some major decisions on the school's
future. Finally, the dean's secretary took action. She let
others within the school know the probable consequences
of getting involved in the battle, reducing the influence of
both combatants at the same time. She was able to do this
because the faculty knew the dean would back her. She had
been there for seventeen years, through three administra-
tions, and had taught the dean everything he knew about
management!

Knowing when and how to act when you are engaged in
battle is a critical skill. You will find you can save yourself,

save others, and reduce the inevitable fallout by acting decisively. Delay is almost always a mistake because it allows your enemies and victims the time to respond in a planned way, rather than defensively. Suppose you and a colleague are engaged in a very heated but sub rosa battle over who is actually going to direct a project. Your colleague undermines your authority with your subordinates by making "suggestions" that reflect his ideas. You are put in a defensive position as you undo his suggestions and reassure your subordinates that you are in charge.

If you seek support from your boss, he is likely to think that you are not competent in solving your own problems. "Why can't you and he work it out? Why involve me?" he will say. The best strategy is to confront your colleague and tell him to stop. Then tell him the consequences of not stopping. Say, "Tim, if you don't stop making counterproductive suggestions, we'll have to call a meeting and bang out the issues publicly. Do you think that would help?" If you wait, Tim will assume that you cannot do anything about his behavior or, worse, that you do not know what to do. If you act decisively, you will be petty but powerful. Remember, your subordinates are watching, and they are going to decide how much to trust and be influenced by you, according to what they see.

How you use the information in this chapter is entirely up to you. However, you will find that there are more risks associated with moving around the power markers in the office than in benevolently trying to increase your influence. Because of the risks involved, you should use information in this chapter only when there is a great deal of power at stake, not out of a fit of pique. The greatest risk is that any attempt may ultimately strengthen your competitor. For instance, in your drive for a promotion you may try to cut your competitor off from information he or she needs. If you are unsuccessful, that person may redouble his/her efforts in order to show you that you made a mistake in trying. You might also provoke retaliation from your target's allies.

WHAT POWER WEAKNESSES ARE

A power weakness is one of three things: a blind spot, the formation of an unstable alliance, or a change in circumstances which changes an individual's position or role. Let us look at these individually. A blind spot forms when someone misjudges his/her reputation, cannot or will not see his/her work realistically, or makes unfounded assumptions about other people's needs and interests.

BLIND SPOTS

In the first case, the person involved has a blind spot about his/her reputation such that he/she is emotional rather than rational. For instance, a boss feels sure he is very well liked by his subordinates. This is not true, but who wants to disillusion him? It would not be a power problem if it involved mere self-delusion. The weakness here is that the boss depends on being liked and uses these feelings as one weapon in his arsenal. He/she believes people cooperate because they like him, not because he has position power.

In tranquil times this is a minor difficulty. The problem occurs when the boss tests that imagined esteem by asking for a special favor. When the subordinate or peer refuses (or just ducks, as is more likely), the boss is forced to face reality. The disillusionment almost always produces cynicism. Just when the boss needs cool judgment, he becomes emotional, thereby undercutting himself. As Don Quixote learned, nothing is more hateful than being forced to look into the mirror of reality.

Another kind of blind spot occurs when someone believes that his/her work is far superior to that of his/her peers. This fantasy flourishes in organizations where performance appraisals are perfunctory or irregularly scheduled. Unless someone's performance is shocking and publicly inadequate, there is no feedback until a serious mistake is made or a crisis occurs. Many small companies do not even have formal appraisal systems. They keep an employee on the job because the owner thinks the business is really one big "family." Not until this person has offended the owner, or has been charged with embezzlement, is he or she likely to be dumped. It is not the owner's style to dismiss for incompetence.

Dismissal or just demotion will be extremely shocking to the person because he/she thought everything was fine. There was no hint of any problem before the event. This makes him/her vulnerable. Other people looking at the situation know rationally that the person has a soft spot. Some may even try to exploit it.

A third power blind spot occurs when people are so involved in the politics of the situation they forget that others share neither their involvement nor their enthusiasm. They assume feelings on the part of others without having checked whether those feelings actually exist or are ever likely to exist. Many have little ambition to move up. They want to earn a living with the least possible effort. To treat these people as enthusiastic participants in the power process is a mistake. They are not, nor do they want to be. Their job-related values are different. To assume that there is a commonality at this level is a mistake. For example, a woman works very hard to impress her boss with her diligence and ambition. It has no effect. Her boss really still prefers nice legs, which she lacks. It never occurred to her that decisions about her career might depend on something other than performance and her desire to move up.

A fourth kind of power blind spot, and a very common one, occurs when someone refuses to accept facts that violate his/her idea of logic. Women are especially prone to this problem. If they hear that something that seems absurd or illogical is going to happen, they will discount the rumor. This makes them vulnerable to logical untruths. For instance, a rumor is circulating that the company will be reorganized. It was reorganized a year ago. Could anyone logically put everyone through that kind of pain again so soon? Logically, no; in reality, yes. By not believing well-founded but bizarre rumors, you cut your planning time and force yourself to react under pressure. That reduces power. When you have a competitor or boss who cannot or will not deal with this type of situation, you can grab power by planning immediately for the probable contingencies.

A fifth kind of blind spot is irrational emotional involvement. Nothing has the ability to make someone as vulnerable in the office as an unreasonable attachment to an employee or colleague; this causes the person not to act in his/her own self-interest. If someone refuses to see that her secretary, while indisputably a lovely person, is not competent and is undermining the department's work, that person is very vulnerable. It also causes a chain reaction. Having defended the secretary once, the boss will almost always have to do it again. She undermines her power by letting people know that she will not negotiate about the secretary, thus forcing others to work around her.

UNSTABLE ALLIANCES

A second kind of weakness develops when people have joined either a weak or a highly unstable alliance. The alliance, which might look tight to an outsider, may be very loosely held together. The tie may be that all agree to oppose someone on a particular issue. There is no tight community of interest among the people. The best example of this is the group drawn together in order to get even with someone for a deeply felt but trivial wrong.

This can happen when a new manager comes into the organization and begins to fire people, reassign jobs, and restructure work assignments. It can happen anytime people feel collectively threatened. As the remaining people circle their wagons, they also ally against the new boss. In the past they have had very different needs and interests, and not much in common. However, now the glue is their strong desire to cause the new boss as many problems as possible. Once they have reduced the boss's power, or gotten rid of him/her, they will go in different directions. They will, once again, compete among themselves.

The alliance may be undermined because no maintenance has been done. The people in it assume that they will, individually and collectively, always feel the same about whatever brought them together in the first place. They do not keep in close enough touch. This is an explosive assumption because without regular contact and interaction the people cannot keep the base of the alliance strong. They will, perhaps without realizing it, drift into other alliances. At the very least they will not be able to gauge each other's reactions.

An alliance may have chinks because most of the people

simply do not like one another. Not only are their interests dissimilar, their personal and professional values and styles are also divergent. Because they feel that way, an otherwise minor disagreement could cause the group to splinter into one or more smaller groups—always a problem with peer group alliances. Unless a need affects each member of the group equally, the desire to compete, along with jealousy or dislike of someone's style, will splinter the group. The larger the group, the more this is true. Suppose ten people are allied in favor of the department adopting flextime. You, the manager, have already decided that the plan the group favors is unworkable. How do you detach some of the ten from their alliance and add them to your group? Remember, you might be able to silence them by command, but you will not be able to keep them from reducing their productivity in retaliation. The only way to detach someone is to show him/her a different view of his/her self-interest (that is, make the person a better offer).

CHANGE IN CIRCUMSTANCE

In addition to the weaknesses that alliances tend to develop, the individual participants often become vulnerable. If you wanted to reduce someone's power, look for the following problems. Always remember, however, that there is a risk in the process of acting on any of these.

1. The relationship with the boss changes. Someone who is quite powerful can be undone because his/her relationship with the boss changes. It is rarely deliberate. Something happens, possibly a falling out over an issue, a change in direction, or an awakening ambition, and suddenly the person no longer has the same influence. The boss may change his/her style or direction and no longer value someone as in the past. The boss's boss may cause a change. These

changes create opportunities for someone to reduce the person's power unless that person immediately shores up the relationship by either changing his/her style or learning to repackage. If someone contemplates changing jobs, it means that the person does not think the relationship can be repaired. When this occurs, that person's power diminishes drastically, and anyone can seize it.

2. The person moved, or is moving, too far from his/her primary group. Someone is not doing his/her relationship maintenance. Some of this person's contacts are tired of it and are open to suggestions concerning joining another group. Lack of maintenance has the same kind of effect on relationships as it does on a car: disastrous.

3. The person has not totally penetrated the organization. There are places, some of them very important, from which the person gets no news. There are entire divisions he or she has never heard from. The person has dismissed certain departments or divisions as unworthy of investigation. This is especially dangerous if one of the neglected areas is a profit center.

4. The person relies on others for too much information. These sources have both a need and a desire to shape the news the person does get. This happens most often in smaller companies when top management develops blind spots because they are concentrating on a particular area.

5. The person is unsure of what she/he wants to happen. Nothing creates power problems as quickly as indecision. Someone who is trying to do something often feels like shouting "gangway" when surrounded by people who really do not understand either the problem or the solution.

THE UNWRITTEN RULES

What are the rules of fair play when you are trying to reduce someone's power? How much can you expect to tickle the formal system without doing yourself any harm? Here are the rules as they are practiced in most places.

1. Except in periods of reorganization, reduction in work force, or merger, or surgery on someone's power, at whatever level, is done through the informal system. You do not want to involve the formal system because everything you do would then become a matter of official record. The most extreme example of this is giving an employee a chance to resign rather than be fired. Officially, the employee resigns and no reason is given. Unofficially, he or she was fired and everyone knows it. The informal system may have made the decision, but it was never shared with the formal system. A memo announcing the resignation will serve as confirmation by the formal system.

2. Reducing power should not be part of any personal action. Do not mix revenge for something that someone did to you with reducing power. If you do, observers will not see the business interest you are trying to protect. They will assume it is all personal. This has the effect of making you seem vindictive and will reduce your trustworthiness with your other allies.

3. If you tell someone what you are doing, you have violated a taboo. Always act alone. The difference between your action and having someone working with you is the difference between an assassin and a mob. The mob inevitably evokes more fear and, in the office, more danger of weakening your other alliances and provoking retaliation.

4. Act decisively. If you are going to do something, pick the right time and then do it. Do not warn through the grapevine. If you do, you will only increase attention and cause others to get involved against you.

STRATEGY PLANNING

Suppose that you and a co-worker are involved in a career-threatening dispute. You are both contending for promotion, but he is spending most of his time telling others about your weaknesses, both real and imagined! The office waits breathlessly for you to respond. You have several choices. You can confront him as we discussed in chapter two. You can retaliate through the grapevine. You can use your allies to carry your story. You can involve your boss or others more powerful than you. You can do nothing.

Before you do anything it is important to measure the risks of each course of action. To do this you will need to list them separately and then brainstorm the possible ways your peer might respond and also the possible fallout.

Strategy	Possible Responses
1. Confrontation	
2. Retaliate/grapevine	
3. Use allies	
4. Involve boss	
5. Do nothing	

Once you have evaluated the risks, it is important to compare them with the value you attach to winning. It is senseless to go for broke over something which, even if attained, is not worth it. Assuming your interest in the promotion is intense, you may believe the risks are worth it. Since you are operating within the formal system, you can recover from a serious setback. You have not been exposed or disciplined in writing. As the climate continues to change and others enter the spotlight, you may find yourself out of the news. Even if people are still discussing your failed coup they will respect you more for trying than those who do nothing to advance their own interests.

11. MAINTAINING POWER

REGINA Frank, a nursing supervisor for a 1,200-bed teaching hospital, had always had excellent relationships with both the physicians and the teaching staff. She was always available to talk about problems over coffee or lunch, easy to reach on the telephone, and eager to participate in some aftershift frivolity. One day she and her husband found themselves practically in litigation when what should have been a simple divorce turned ugly. She began to spend coffee breaks and lunches on the telephone with her lawyer. At the end of the shift she rushed to her car to head home and get on with straightening out her personal life. One day her boss, the vice-president of nursing services, approached her. She said that she had heard Regina was not doing her job. She was not available. People did not think she was "on top of things." Since Regina was working as hard as she had on the technical parts of her job, she quickly realized what had happened. She had been seriously neglecting her power maintenance.

Now that you have established a power base, how do you hold on to that power and influence? It is not as if you can lock your relationships away, embalm them, or cement what you have worked so hard to acquire. Relationships occur in a dynamic environment and keeping them strong requires regular maintenance. In this chapter we will present a plan for maintaining power that does not demand your full-time attention. Maintenance usually requires between twenty and fifty percent of the time you have invested in building your relationships. Since you have invested so much time already, going into a maintenance mode will seem highly desirable, almost like a vacation! You will soon find that it is not a question of whether you should or should not maintain your position as much as what techniques work best and when you should use them. If you do not do regular maintenance, you will always be in a building phase.

WHAT IS MAINTENANCE?

The basis of power, once you have built a base, is relationships. In its simplest form, maintenance is the process of keeping both internal and external relationships warm and firm. You are maintaining power successfully if, when you call for information or a favor, the person you call responds readily. She/he does not need to be enthusiastic, just willing and able to help. You have spent considerable time building both influencing and negotiating relationships with those you work with and for, as well as with those who work for you. You do not need to be in continuous touch with all of these people. That would leave you without time to do your job, much less add new contacts to an ever-increasing circle. It must be ever-increasing since there is always some attrition as some of your contacts move out of town, change careers, or simply drop out of your network. The object is to minimize contact while retaining enough influence to get what you want, and retaining enough trust to be able to negotiate whenever it becomes necessary. For example, it is unlikely that someone you see every other year is going to enter into delicate negotiations with you unless you do considerable rapport building first.

Maintenance also involves regularly using your power to trade information and favors. If you have no mutual interest with someone, then that person is not subject to either building or maintenance. It may be more difficult than you would think to recognize one stage from the other. Occasionally, you must test the water to make sure the relationships are still there. For example, if you once needed help from someone in housekeeping, got it, and have not seen your contact since, the relationship is tenuous. It is especially true if your need for help from that department is always going to be infrequent. Why pursue that connection when you cannot help the other person regularly or benefit from her help? Unless the other person can see how you and she could have a mutually beneficial relationship, she is out of your network.

INTERNAL RELATIONSHIPS

If you see peers in a different division of your company four times a year, do you need more contact in order to keep those relationships going? Depending on how competitive you are with those people, three other contacts, between face-to-face meetings, will keep all of you up to date on each other's activities. If those relationships are shaky, for instance all of you are competing for the same thing, you need to have a five-minute, once-a-week, how-are-you-what's-on-the-street discussion with them. Keeping internal contacts warm means making monthly decisions on how often you will meet. Everything depends on your needs and theirs at the time.

Here are some questions to ask yourself as you begin a maintenance program.

1. What do the people you need contact with have at stake in keeping the relationship going? If all of the people in your network have similar needs, it is much easier to maintain your relationships. They will be working to keep in contact with you, too. If, however, some of your important sources are political ostriches, and every office has some, you will find yourself working much harder to keep in touch. These people refuse to acknowledge that they need others in any way. Some actually believe that your continued good will and cooperation come with the job description. If too much good will is assumed, you will need to correct this impression tactfully.

If a manager in a public accounting firm needs regular contact with a partner who is going to "sponsor" her in a partnershp election, her stake is clearly greater than the partner's. She will have to work quite hard in order to keep the relationship professionally close. If she worked directly for the partner, the partner would have some stake in her performance and would usually work at the relationship, too. If she works for someone else, she will have the burden of promoting and maintaining involvement with the partner as well as protecting and promoting her career with her direct boss.

2. Is the relationship competitive or complimentary? Your

relationship with your boss is not competitive (hopefully); your relationships with your peers are. You will have to spend more time on peer relationships, reassuring your peers that you are not moving too quickly, doing favors for them and letting them reciprocate, and making yourself generally agreeable. You do the same kind of thing with a boss but not as aggressively. Your object in competitive relationships is to keep your peers from undermining you. The best way to do this is to have regular contact with them. They will hesitate to bad-mouth you if they see you on a regular basis; it would be embarrassing for them to do so.

3. Are the people with whom you network extraordinarily needy? Are they people who require more ego stroking and more reassurance than you judge to be normal? If you have surrounded yourself (or have been involuntarily surrounded) with delicate or damaged egos, you will have a more difficult job than if most of your contacts are professionally and personally self-confident. Still, even if it means more work, it is not a bad position to be in. After all, there is nothing better for keeping relationships in the office going than sustained mutual need. Even if someone else could meet the same need, it's usually easier and less time consuming to maintain ongoing relationships than to build new ones.

4. Are many of your relationships symbiotic? That is, are you meeting each other's needs to the extent that it would be difficult or impossible to replace each other? For instance, it is unlikely that you would have to do much maintenance on a relationship which keeps both you and a peer performing at a high level. Your relationship with your boss should be symbiotic. The word processing supervisor and the partners in an accounting firm will both work at maintaining a good relationship with one another because this relationship

is vital to each of their careers. A secretary will need to work at building and keeping a relationship with the word processing supervisor because her stake in the relationship is greater than the supervisor's.

OUTSIDE RELATIONSHIPS

Keeping up your external relationships is somewhat more difficult than keeping up your internal ones because you are not likely to run into someone who works across town in the company men's room. You will also work either harder or less intensely on these relationships, depending on what you expect to gain from them. There are different levels of maintenance, and each one requires a different level of personal effort. It is only pragmatic to make these distinctions and budget your time accordingly. If you don't, the maintenance task itself will seem overwhelming.

1. Pure maintenance means that you are neither job hunting outside your company nor in internal political trouble. You are simply keeping in contact with (keeping warm) all of the people you know in the trade and professional societies, those you have met through others and quasi-social contacts. You only need to see them or speak to them three or four times a year. For example, you will be sure to call several times a year any people that you do not run into at meetings. If you hear anything about them or their companies, pass this information along via telephone, and then count that as a contact. You may get five or six people together three times a year for a drink after work, just for a general sharing of news. In pure maintenance you only add new contacts to replace those who move out of the work force or out of town.

2. Active maintenance is necessary when your company is in trouble. You believe that you may be job hunting in

the near future, so you begin to raise your visibility in your networking organizations. You may, if the problem occurs in the early spring, run for the board of directors of your favorite association. At the very least you will be hounding the membership chair for a supplemental list of members who have joined since the directory was published. (If you are really interested in getting to know the membership, it would be good to volunteer either for membership or directory chair.) One of the ways to identify people who are gearing up for job hunting is to note who asks for directory updates. Members who are not actively job hunting, or at least preparing to look, often forget that such updates are issued. If your association does not do this formally, ask for a photocopy of the names of new members who have joined since the directory was published.

At this point you will try to meet, or at least nod to, everyone who is at the monthly meetings. You may even begin calling members who you think have different contacts from yours about every two weeks, just to see if they have heard of any openings. This is preparatory to a full-scale job hunt which may involve actually canvassing the entire membership, as well as calling all business contacts. In the active maintenance stage, you usually try to add ten new names per month to your existing contacts list.

3. Aggressive maintenance is the actual canvassing of everyone you know outside of your own organization. This happens most often when someone believes that there is a finite, even if unknown, time before he/she will be out of his/her current organization. Aggressive maintenance is part of a full-scale, immediate job hunt and usually calls for weekly contact with everyone on an ever-expanding list. This is not truly maintenance; it is a blending of maintenance with building, for you are adding many new people to your

list. The main goal of this type of maintenance is to get the names of and call twenty to thirty new people a week. Obviously this is practically a full-time job. However, since research shows that it takes about two hundred contacts to produce ten live job leads, this is the quickest and smartest way to move. In the time that it would take to answer a want ad and be told that you do not meet a company's needs, you could be going to work someplace new if you had been canvassing.

DEVELOPING THE DAILY PLAN

Your goal in developing a maintenance plan is to structure it so that you do three or four things every day as part of your normal work routine. If you portion out your maintenance tasks on a daily basis, you need spend no more than fifteen or twenty minutes per day on telephone calls. The key is organization. The best system involves the use of a yearly calendar marked off in fifteen-minute segments. We like Day-Timer, Inc., only because you can buy the system in different sizes with different amounts of writing space. The Day-Timer is also very portable (it tucks into a handbag or briefcase); this is very important because you do not want any part of your system lying around the office. You definitely do not want your peers to figure out what you are doing. You cannot prevent them from buying Day-Timer, but why show them how to maximize the system as well?

You will enter in the calendar the names of people you want to contact several months prior to when you will actually need to make the calls. For instance, if you need to talk four times a year to a peer at a competitive company, you will enter the name and telephone number in your calendar on four different days. If you need to have coffee on a monthly basis with a colleague in your own company, you can enter his/her name on a particular day and declare the second Tuesday of the month "his day." You will do this with everyone, internally as well as externally, with whom you need to touch base regularly.

If you are actively job hunting, these calls become even more important. You may spend several hours per day on regular telephone calls to contacts who are most likely to hear of openings in your field. As you talk to each one, enter their name and telephone number in your calendar on a day two weeks hence. Always enter both the name and the telephone number. If you do not, you will be tempted to skip a strictly routine call because of the time it would take to look up a telephone number. It is also easier to carry around one book instead of two. Makes this process a "no-brainer." If you are seriously job hunting, you have enough troubles already. Do not put up unnecessary road blocks.

If your company is in crisis or being taken over, or if management is reorganizing, you will have to make even more calls. Such calls must now be made more frequently if you want to keep both internal and external contacts warm. In turbulent times it is not unusual for people to talk to their contacts several times a day, either on the telephone or in person. If that is your situation, remember that while you need not enter on the calendar the name of someone with whom you talk every day, you may need some reminders of less frequent but still very important contacts. There is no respite from this at any level.

How does this relationship maintenance help you in power building? Relationship maintenance does two things: It gives you some sense of control by keeping your information current, and people watching you will see you getting the news on a regular basis. They will know you are friendly with a great many people, and they will deal with you differently because of it. After all, people are the ultimate source of power.

FAVOR SAVERS

In addition to maintaining contacts, you need to keep track of the favors you do for others and also the favors done for you. Whom do you owe? If you are going to be powerful, many people must owe you and you them. You should keep track in your calendar of who did something for you as well as who owes you, so that you can flip through your calendar at will for a quick inventory. For example, if you have readjusted your schedule twice in order to help a colleague on a rush assignment, that person definitely owes you a favor. You should find a way for him/her to repay you within six months of your having provided help. The meaning of your effort will fade significantly and will soon be worth less in a trade if you are not fairly prompt. You could remind your trading partner when you ask to be repaid, but it is easier and more tactful to ask for help quickly.

Occasionally you will run into people who deliberately do not pay back favors. They expect you to do favors for them and give to them forever without their ever having to respond in kind. They may think that because you want things to go smoothly in the office you will not make a fuss over nonreciprocity. They may be challenging you, to see if you will really confront them on this issue. They may also be terminally selfish. Disabuse them of the notion that they have found a fountain of freebies. Let them know immediately what you expect, or you will find that they will always use you.

If someone owes you more than two favors, it is up to you to withhold help the next time he/she asks for it. Tell him/her specifically why you are refusing. Say, "I'd like to help, but I've noticed that you never return the favor. We can't help each other unless it's mutual." Then wait. At a later date, ask the person again for a favor. If the person does not change his/her behavior, there is no rational reason why you should keep the relationship going. Drop the person as a trading partner and replace him/her with someone who is more interested in equality, someone whose needs are more compatible with yours. If you cannot entirely drop the person—say it is a peer with whom you must regularly cooperate—minimize your involvement with this person, and then let the grapevine know why.

Occasionally you will find someone who will try to intimidate you into cooperation while simultaneously withholding his/her help. This person can either be disciplined through the grapevine: "Jack isn't very good at cooperating; he's not a team player." Or you can confront him personally: "Tell me, Jack, why don't you ever return the favor when someone helps you out?" Confrontation may be the better way if the person truly believes that the others will not make a fuss because he/she intimidates them.

CREATING OPPORTUNITIES

An excellent power maintenance strategy is to do favors for people who aren't part of your primary networking groups.

Have you recently seen a laudatory newspaper clip about someone you have heard of but don't know personally? If the person works for the same company, send him/her a memo. If the person is outside the company, send a hand-written note with the clip. Senior executives love this. They are always sure that no one in the company but the public relations people sees stories about them. You, by forwarding the clip, are opening the lines of communication to someone who may be useful to you later. That connection could help you to cement other present relationships just by people knowing that it exists.

Never miss a company-sponsored function. Circulate and meet everyone. Have you ever seen a politician working a meeting room right before an election? The politician says a few words to everyone present. You need to do the same thing, but a little less conspicuously. There are few people in your company who could not help you if provided with the proper incentive to do so. It may seem strange, but few people see company events as the power building opportunities they really are. Company events are considered wildly successful if there is ten to thirty percent participation. In very small companies fifty percent participation would thrill management. Why, then, are the people who do attend grouped in their tight little clusters? They do that every day. Not one person has moved off the dime. These events provide the perfect opportunity for networking with new people and for breaking out of routine information clusters. They also allow you to test your theories about which alliances are still strong and which, if any, are splintering.

ANTICIPATING PROBLEMS

You should always be conscious of the fact that you are being observed, often in a predatory manner, by your co-workers at every level. Be ready for problems, even in a good maintenance program. For instance, a peer may decide you are crowding him/her and become aggressive. As long as you have been maintaining power with everyone else, this will be a relatively minor problem. If you anticipate these roadblocks to effective maintenance, you will be able to eliminate most of them.

1. Your peers may decide that you have excessively raised the level of expected effort. Your maintenance effort with them must now include low visibility; until you exercise your power for a specific purpose, no one should be entirely sure that you even have any. Flaunting power with peers threatens them and invites them to develop an alliance against you. Should this happen, reestablish your relationships with them on a one-to-one basis, thereby detaching each person from the alliance as a whole.

2. You get bored making calls or arranging coffee breaks and luncheon meetings. Boredom is an inevitable part of the maintenance process. Seeing people you do not particularly care for is tedious. Dry periods, when nothing seems to be happening, can sap both your commitment to the process and your energy.

You have to bear up under this kind of stress. Even very powerful people cannot choose to be only with interesting people, nor can they schedule the news. One technique that may help you is to learn how to turn your mind off while simultaneously maintaining an expression of enraptured attention. It also helps to remember that you are a power builder, not a personality critic. If you want to maintain the power that you have worked so hard to build, you will have to follow through on these calls. The more contacts you maintain during breaks and lunches, the less you will need to do after work. The mere thought of free evenings should encourage you.

3. Things are changing rapidly in your organization, and you fall behind in your maintenance. If you are so snowed under with work that it is going to be several months before you have the time to make any calls or see any people outside of your primary group, you must change your game plan quickly. Immediately strengthen your departmental and divisional networking. Be sure you are in touch with several competitors' networks and at least one of your trade/professional societies. If you have contact each month with at least ten people within the organization and twenty outside of it, you can tread water in that fashion for several months. You will not be able to job hunt or work on a promotion, but you also will not have to start at ground zero again when your work load decreases.

4. You are going through a personal crisis which saps your energy and leaves you longing for solitude, not more contact with people. Keep your departmental and divisional contacts warm. You can, if you truly must, let your involvement in outside groups diminish until you are able to deal with them. Six months without those contacts, however, and for all practical purposes you will be starting over again.

5. Your boss objects to the time you spend networking, even though it is not taking any time away from your

work and you are not doing it under his nose. You have been clever enough not to give anyone anything to talk about. However, your boss senses that you are doing more work in influence and power building than he/she would like you to do. If your boss becomes concerned, you are going to have to do more afterwork socializing. If you do not immediately reduce your visibility within the office, you may soon be out on the street. A boss who mentions networking to you, especially if he/she benefits from the information you gather, feels very threatened. Although it may be an irrational feeling, it is a very real one. Lower your visibility immediately. Spend one or two coffee breaks at your desk. Have lunch outside the office with noncompany people twice a week, and then talk about it. If these people are old college pals, so much the better. They may be contacts, but they are old pals first. Never lie about this. If you are asked, tell the truth. If you are asked for names, mention them. If you were meeting a headhunter, give the name but do not identify him/her as such. You and the headhunter might have been innocently networking, or you might have been sharing names of your needy friends in other companies.

Never forget that your competitors are often lax in maintenance. They may decide to let things go "just this one time," or they may skip a professional meeting for a new movie or dinner with a friend. Given the greater effort which you have put in, why shouldn't you have the greater reward?

If Mary wants that information, let her negotiate for it. If she feels you are getting ahead, let her say so. Take hints selectively.

THE BOTTOM LINE

Will there ever be a lunch hour you can call your own? Is the rest of your life destined to be mortgaged to contact building and maintenance? If you want to build and maintain power, the answer is a definite yes. You might consider the alternatives, however. Either you take control of and maintain relationships, or you will be buffeted by those who do. There is no middle ground. If it is any consolation, doing maintenance will eventually become almost automatic. You allocate the time and, unless you are actively job hunting, the process will become second nature to you.

A few compensations for your efforts, although not immediately obvious, are very important. Even if you previously did not see yourself as a people person, you will become one after regularly doing this. You will find that your skills in dealing easily with people will develop and improve with regular use. At first it may seem difficult to think up new ways to cement relationships, but after you have been at it for several years, it seems as normal a part of life as brushing your teeth, rotating the tires on the car, or mowing the lawn. You will begin to sniff out opportunities which others not so finely attuned will miss. The payoff will be that, since you are there first, there is less competition. People will assume that your power is either inborn or the result of luck.

Never forget that your competitors are often lax in maintenance. They may decide to let things go "just this one time," or they may skip a professional meeting for a new movie or dinner with a friend. Given the greater effort which you have put in, why shouldn't you have the greater reward?

EPILOGUE

As you reflect on what you have read about power building, several things should be very clear.

1. You are in charge if you take charge. The theme has been that you will be what you choose to be. If you want to be powerful, you have the tools to do so.

2. You are always going to be at risk. If you are powerful, someone may want to bump you off. You will spend some time looking over your shoulder.

3. By implication, these techniques would work socially as well as in a work situation. If you have social ambitions, you can use the same game to build power socially.

One final caveat. Never violate your personal ethics. For some reason people can sense when you are ethically over-extended, and they often move in on you at that point. Do not get so enamored of the process that you forget power is only a means to an end. It isn't an end in itself. Here's why. If you decide to build power for the sheer joy of being powerful, you will never have enough. You will always be thinking of ways to become more powerful. That is going to negatively affect your work satisfaction. It will also endanger your job tenure because you will get so wrapped up in power building, especially building relationships, that you will neglect your job. Keeping a sense of perspective is the most important test of your maturity and sophistication as a power builder. Good luck!